The Adventures
of
Colonel Daffodil

by the same author,
Balkan Blue (Leo Cooper, 2000)

The Adventures
of
Colonel Daffodil

Balkan Beginnings, Memorable Travels
and Forgotten Conflicts

Roy Redgrave

LEO COOPER

First published in Great Britain in 2006 by
LEO COOPER
an imprint of
Pen & Sword Books Ltd
47 Church Street
Barnsley
South Yorkshire
S70 2AS

Copyright Roy Redgrave, 2007

ISBN 978-1-84415-525-5

A CIP catalogue record for this book is
available from the British Library

Typeset in 11/13 Plantin by Concept, Huddersfield, West Yorkshire
Printed and bound in England by Biddles Ltd

Pen & Sword Books Ltd incorporates the Imprints of
Pen & Sword Aviation, Pen & Sword Maritime, Pen & Sword Military,
Wharncliffe Local History, Pen & Sword Select,
Pen & Sword Military Classics and Leo Cooper

For a complete list of Pen & Sword titles please contact
PEN & SWORD BOOKS LIMITED
47 Church Street, Barnsley, South Yorkshire, S70 2AS, England
E-mail: enquiries@pen-and-sword.co.uk
Website: www.pen-and-sword.co.uk

CONTENTS

ACKNOWLEDGEMENTS

I am indebted to Douglas Liversidge, Commander Angus Erskine RN and Sir Alexander Glen, who have all died in recent years, for telling me about their experiences in the High Arctic.

I am grateful to Olav Farnes for his recollections and to Tom Hartman for his painstaking checking of Inuit and Romanian spellings and for the presentation of this book. I have been encouraged by the enthusiasm and sage advice of my publisher Brigadier Henry Wilson.

My heartfelt thanks for the memory of Ioana Hart, my sister, who checked the first six chapters before she died a few months ago. My constant solace throughout the years it has taken me to decide to conclude this book has been entirely thanks to the persuasion, patience and understanding shown by my wife, Valerie, to whom I dedicate this book.

PREFACE

Daffodil was a miniature Pekinese bitch who weighed less than a kilogram. She had bandy legs and one bright eye. The other had been removed by a mean stable cat in the first week that she joined the Household Cavalry Mounted Regiment at Hyde Park Barracks in London. She always preceded me on my morning tour of inspection of the stables. Neat piles of steaming manure and straw bedding were laid out in the yard to dry in the sun. This was then used again, thus saving the Quartermaster money. Troopers might be resting on their brooms when invariably someone, like an alert African meerkat, would shout, 'Eyes down, here comes Daffodil', thus warning dozing troopers of their Commanding Officer's imminent arrival and the stable yard would suddenly become a scene of great activity.

Daffodil's friend was called Hannibal, a much-loved drum horse of the Blues, whose hoof alone was enormous. When he died his hooves were shod with silver horseshoes and turned into handsome inkwells. Much later the regiment was horrified to discover that five such hooves had been created, and decided, in order to avoid disappointment, that it was best to say nothing. Daffodil lived for many years and her gravestone stands among the daffodils in a garden in the village of Warmwell in Dorset. To some people it seems I had already become Colonel Daffodil. Fifteen years later, when I was Major General, Brigade of Gurkhas, Hong Kong, this may have changed to General Daffodil Sahib.

I was brought up in Romania. I did not go to school until I was nine years old, in 1934, when I left home for the first time and was sent to Lambrook, a boarding school in Berkshire. Five years later, during the summer holidays, which were spent beside the Black Sea, the Second World War began. I was sent back to England, to Sherborne School, in October 1939. It was to be six years before I saw any of my family again.

Having missed out on the early years of schooling, I realized I knew absolutely nothing about English history except the story of

1

Robin Hood. It was not until I became a Wolf Cub at Lambrook and was taught how to light a campfire that I was also taught the history of the Union Jack. I was keen that Romania's history should not be forgotten, so I was frequently given to outbursts, standing up in class for Romania, based on the crumbs of information gleaned from my Romanian mother. It influenced my thinking. I suppose I had a chip on my shoulder.

The corruption which existed in Romania at all levels, and still lingers on, was not revealed to me until I was much older. It seemed perfectly normal that my father was obliged to bribe the gendarmes to allow the distillation of plums to continue, provided they each received a bottle of plum brandy. The still was well-hidden behind the coach house at the bottom of the garden. The smell, however, was very strong when it was working.

Our big American Buick motor car was taxed by weight. This meant that it turned up at the taxation office without a spare wheel, with no back seat or tools, and an empty fuel tank.

I have described my life up to leaving the Army in a biography called *Balkan Blue*. The story continues with the Romanian background to my family history and the adventures I have enjoyed during some of my travels.

Little-known battles were fought in the High Arctic in which a handful of men survived in the harsh climate and against heavy odds. The Cold War in all its forms has occupied much of my life. My admiration goes to those local leaders such as village policemen who have to make big decisions, which, to us in our ignorance, may seem trivial. Is the ice strong enough to take a sledge? Does he let the smuggler go free and risk losing his job or does he arrest him and get a stone through his window?

PART I
1861–1919

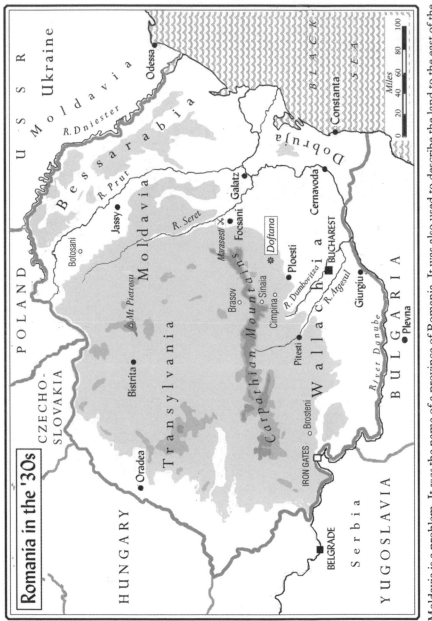

Romania is a problem. It *was* the name of a province of Romania. It was also used to describe the land to the east of the River Dniester. This is now a separate country called Moldova. Several maps of Romania in the 1930s show Moldavia as being both to the east and west of the Rivers Prut and Dniester.

Chapter 1

DANUBE DEBUT

My Romanian grandfather, Mihai Capsa, was aged twenty-one when, long before dawn on 22 February, 1866, he joined a group of officers who forced their way into the royal palace in Bucharest. There was no bloodshed and complete surprise was achieved. Not unexpectedly, they found their ruler in bed with a lady whose notoriety was such that he was obliged to sign a document of abdication which the intruders had thoughtfully brought with them. One wonders what on earth had been going on in the royal bed-chamber that proved so unacceptable to the exasperated officials of the fledgling country.

Nevertheless, within a very short time Colonel Alexander Cuza was on his way to Giurgiu on the Danube with a small travelling escort of cavalry to make sure he caught the next steamship back to Germany.

Six years earlier, in 1860, Moldavia and Wallachia had been granted independence within the Ottoman Empire. Both princi-palities chose the same man to be ruler and thus achieved an un-complicated union to create a new Romania. Michael the Brave had tried to achieve this in 1600 and was sentenced to death by the Turks for daring to challenge their authority.

Colonel Alexander Cuza had been a popular choice to be the first ruler in 1859. Well aware of his own shortcomings, he warned his people, 'Gentlemen, I fear you will not be satisfied with me'. Never-theless, he started well. He removed all traces of feudalism, which still bound peasant farmers to their landlords. They were given plots of land based on the number of cattle they possessed. He secularized the Greek Orthodox monasteries which substantially increased the revenues to the State. This done, he decided to enjoy himself. He chose to ignore the corruption, favouritism, fraud and general inept-itude of his officials, which resulted in none of his reforms ever being

5

successfully carried out. Very soon the new nation that had made such a promising start was heading towards economic disaster. Hence the dawn raid on the palace and his departure up the Danube.

Romania, then, was a difficult place to reach overland. There was no railway and the roads were awful. The only way to reach Bucharest from Central Europe in any comfort was down the River Danube. The Danube Steamship Company (*Donau Dampfschiffart Gesellschaft*) had been formed in 1829 by two British engineers.

There were many hazards, especially where the river breaks through the Carpathian Mountains at the 'Iron Gates'. Negotiating the turbulent rapids, whirlpools and submerged rocks required ships' captains with steady nerves. In winter the river remained frozen for up to two months. In summer the water level could drop so much that cargoes had to be off-loaded downstream to be collected later.

It is interesting to note that of the 1,190 vessels which travelled regularly between 1885 and 1895, the British owned 738. There were very few towns on the Romanian bank of the river because it flooded up to 15 miles inland, creating swamps in which millions of mosquitoes bred. The nearest landing point to Bucharest was Giurgiu where travellers gave up the comforts of the ship for a horse-drawn carriage which took two days to complete the journey.

Bucharest was founded by a legendary shepherd called Bucur who wandered across the plain with his family and flocks until he reached the River Dimbovitza where he set up camp. Bucur is said to have built a small church with a mushroom belfry. In so doing, he showed himself to be much more energetic than many of his successors. My Romanian great-grandfather was called Bucur or Bucus, a name supposed to have Albanian origins meaning Joy.

After Cuza's departure a distinguished diplomat, Ion Bratianu, visited all the great European royal houses looking for a suitable successor. His choice was Prince Karl of Hohenzollern-Sigmaringen, aged twenty-seven. The Romanian people accepted Prince Karl in a plebiscite in April 1866. However, the Great Powers, meeting in Berlin, would not allow Bratianu, by then the Romanian Prime Minister, to attend the meeting. They decided by four votes to three that Romania's next ruler must be a Romanian.

Bratianu chose to ignore their decision and the young Prince asked the German Chancellor Otto von Bismark for his advice. He told him not to worry, but just 'resign your commission and take a holiday on the Danube'. So Karl slipped into Austria under a false name and booked a second-class ticket on a Danube steamer. On arrival in Bucharest, he was invited to address the National Assembly as Prince Carol I. His speech, delivered in French, was stirring and politically sound: 'On setting foot on this hallowed soil I have become a Romanian ... citizen today, tomorrow, if need be, a soldier. I shall share with you both good and bad fortune. Trust in me as I trust in you.'

It was a good start to a reign which was to last forty-eight years. Any visitor must have been dismayed at the shoddy condition of the capital city. The River Dimbovitza was an open sewer. Citizens had to pick their way through mud, puddles and filth. There were no public lavatories and animals were slaughtered in the open.

The Prince was escorted to his new home by General Golescu. He could hardly believe his eyes when he saw the dilapidated condition of the 'Royal Palace'. It was a long two-storey building which looked onto a small gypsy encampment, with wagons and hobbled horses. The Prince, who had just resigned his commission in the 2nd Prussian Dragoon Guards, must have been profoundly depressed by his Guard of Honour, but their lack of smartness may have been due to having had to wait three hours for him to arrive. As he inspected his soldiers, bare-footed children, chickens and pigs scattered noisily ahead of him.

My grandfather, Mihai, had been discouraged from joining the army by his brother Theodore, a serving officer. Theodore probably pointed out that they were equipped with many different weapons, all obsolete and quite useless. There was no standard military uniform. Soldiers wore their own ragged clothing or cast-off tunics bought from different countries. Training had been left to the whims of instructors who were mercenaries. No wonder the army was demoralized.

Carol faced one big problem: there were no banks in Romania. This meant that moneylenders, mostly Jewish, had great power and consequently there was much anti-Jewish feeling in the country.

There was pilfering and corruption in every department. Only 1,000 out of 3,000 villages had a school. The dead hand of the Ottoman Empire, of which Romania was still a satellite, stifled every initiative Carol made towards achieving independence. The Turks had complained to the Great Powers about his accession and, because they had not even bothered to reply, a Turkish Army now deployed along the south bank of the Danube. Carol decided to take another look at his army. His jaundiced opinion of their fighting potential was justified when a battalion mutinied at the prospect of going to war with useless muskets. The Prince wisely took a steamer from the Black Sea port of Constanta to touch his cap to the Sultan in Constantinople and to assure him of his loyalty, albeit temporary. The Sultan was friendly, possibly because of the Prince's influential German friends.

That crisis solved, Carol decided to return to Germany to seek a wife. The first time he met Elizabeth von Wied he proposed, She was twenty-five, he was thirty and in a hurry. This may have been the high point of their relationship, which got progressively worse. They married within a month, took the steamer down the Danube and then travelled on the new railway from Giurgiu to Bucharest. They were greeted by a 101-gun salute, with curious crowds lining the streets. Sadly, a wave of anti-German feeling was developing, which was directed at the unfortunate German-born Prince and his bride.

When France was attacked by Germany in 1870, public opinion was entirely on the side of the French. Carol's personal sympathies probably lay with his native country. The army in which my grand-father was now serving suppressed an attack on the German colony in Bucharest. In despair, Carol summoned his Regency Council and offered to hand over the government of the country to them. Not surprisingly, they were horrified at having to risk their own reputations and begged him to stay.

The Bulgarians revolted against the Turks in 1876 and became victims of the most terrible atrocities. Romania hoped to stay neutral, but Turkey expected its vassal province to support them. Russia was angry because Romania showed so little enthusiasm for the Slav cause.

Carol hoped that the Turks would offer concessions which would give Romania greater independence, but they refused, so the Russian army was provided with stores and railway transport in return for payment in gold. The Russian advance guard deployed slowly on the Danube, but their commander, Grand Duke Nicholas, was reluctant to leave the fleshpots of Bucharest. Two Turkish gunboats were sunk by mines and shore-based torpedoes, while the remainder were driven back.

Eventually the Russians built a bridge and crossed into Bulgaria. They soon ran into trouble, losing thousands of men in foolhardy attacks. In June the Grand Duke appealed to the Romanians for help, but there was no liaison whatsoever between the two armies.

He tried again in July and sent a personal telegram to Carol: 'At the Romanian Headquarters, wherever that happens to be. The Turks have massed their main strength at Plevna and are crushing us. Pray make a strong demonstration and if possible cross the Danube.'

He sent another telegram on 21 August: 'When can you cross? Do so as soon as possible.' The Russians must have been pretty desperate because they offered to make Carol Supreme Commander of the Allied Forces.

Carol acted swiftly, leading his small army of 140,000 men, by now well-equipped and well-trained, into battle at Plevna. In a brilliant assault the redoubt of Grivitza was seized and the Turkish Commander-in-Chief, Osman Pasha, was captured. Lieutenant Capsa, my grandfather, with a sword in hand and a yellow plume in his hat, ran uphill to storm the ramparts unscathed.

At the Peace Treaty the Russians refused to withdraw from Bessarabia, which had been awarded to Romania after the Crimean War. The Romanians complained bitterly to the Great Powers, but to no avail.

Furthermore, they were ordered to give equal rights to all foreigners, including Jews, allowing them to own property and become Romanian nationals.

When this news reached Bucharest the unfortunate Carol was faced with the prospect of a rebellion. That Jews, to whom most people were in debt, might have a say in the Government was too much. Yet if he failed to implement the measures, then Jewish financiers in the West might withdraw their support for the projects he still hoped to complete. In the event the Romanian government proposed such a complicated bureaucratic procedure, which required an Act of Parliament for each application by a Jew for citizenship, that absolutely nothing happened. Finally, the exasperated Great Powers insisted that Romania take immediate action. About 900 Jews who had fought in the Army were given Romanian nationality and everybody appeared satisfied.

In spite of these setbacks Romania was now a military power and Carol decided that it must become a Kingdom. Only the Italians, their Latin cousins, gave unqualified support. The French and British took some persuading, while Bismark refused to allow independence until Romania had repaid every single mark owing from the railway construction. Eventually they recognized her right to independence and Carol was crowned King in May 1881. The coronation was carried out with as much splendour as the small nation could muster. My grandfather, now a captain, lined the Calea Victorei with his company. It was fitting that the crown should have been made from Turkish guns captured at Plevna.

King Carol was concerned that he had no son. His wife Elizabeth, also known as Carmen Sylva, was considered unlikely to bear another child; a daughter had died aged four. So once again they looked to Germany for a suitable young man. They were attracted to Carol's nephew, Prince Ferdinand of Hohenzollern-Sigmaringen, who was at school in Dusseldorf. In 1893 he married Marie, Queen Victoria's granddaughter, who gave birth to Carol II. This did little to endear her to Elizabeth, who had been sent back to Germany because she had plotted to get Ferdinand married to her Romanian favourite, Helene Varescu, instead of the English girl.

By 1895 much had been done to make Bucharest a modern city. Three main avenues were laid out: Lipscani as a shopping street, Vacaresci residential and Calea Victorei right through the centre. My mother's family, the Rallets, lived at number 108 until they were driven out by the Communists in 1946. There was now fresh drinking water and a proper sewage system. There were horse-drawn trams and every possibility that advanced electric trams might soon be installed. In the city centre public buildings were being repaired and five modern hotels were built, in one of which I was born in 1925, the Hotel Athene Palace (now the Hilton).

King Carol's greatest structural achievement was a railway bridge over the Danube at Cernavoda. It connected Bucharest to Constanta on the Black Sea. The railway line included 30 kilometres of viaducts and small bridges built by the British. The French built a bridge high above the Danube. The number of foreigners in Romania increased. They were quick to seize every opportunity to make money. The needs of the Army attracted Americans who set up a corned-beef factory, Greeks who opened a macaroni mill, Germans who started a candle and soap works, Austrians who made uniforms and army blankets and the French who turned out buttons and badges.

In Bucharest alone, out of a population of 280,000, there were 53,000 aliens and 43,200 Jews. There were Greeks and Armenians in the large cities, Turks and Bulgarians mainly in Dobruja, Serbs to the west along the Danube, a large German community in the Carpathians and a troublesome group of Magyars in Transylvania, but the largest minority, spread through out the country and who had no foreign power to champion their cause, were the Gypsies.

Another colourful minority were the Lipovans, Russian exiles known as 'The Old Believers'. They drove horse-drawn taxi carriages in summer and sledges in winter. Easily distinguishable by their round fur hats, they sat high above their coach horses. They wore long overcoats reaching down to their ankles.

By now 20 per cent of the nation was Jewish; in Bucharest there were five synagogues. This caused universal concern, the bitter feeling against them was probably due to envy. The Jewish birth rate was higher than any other section of the population. The Jews held monopolies in the retail trade. They owned great timber forests in Moldavia, they owned the wine and spirit shops and were well established as moneylenders. Their commercial success was due to the fact that they were far better educated than the Romanian peasants and much more quick-witted. The Jews seemed to avoid all manual labour, possibly because they were not strong and were always able to pay someone to do the work. Yet without Jewish enterprise and money Romania would have stagnated much longer, a legacy of the Ottoman Empire. Sadly, the Jews became too successful and too numerous, bringing upon themselves in years to come unjustified persecution.

Chapter 2

DISASTROUS DIPLOMACY

The ceremony of Changing the Guard at the Royal Palace was a spectacle not noted for its military precision, more a social occasion for spectators and participants alike. When she was five years old my mother, Micheline Capsa, was taken by Lola, the nursemaid, to watch the guard mounting. It was a brave sight as the soldiers, headed by a brass band, came into view carrying their rifles at the slope and swinging their arms vigorously across their bodies. They were very much aware that all eyes were on them and they tried hard to keep their dressing and in step.

To girls like Lola the uniform was irresistible, a dark blue tunic with red facings, lots of gold braid, white trousers and black boots, tall shako hats with bright red pompoms. As the soldiers marched along they chatted to the girls who ran alongside. They even managed to kiss hands and blow kisses to distant admirers. The young officers naturally tried to show a little more decorum and dignity, but they too looked around during the protracted ceremonial and if they saw a friend in the crowd would bow stiffly and salute.

It was a pleasant way to spend a morning, followed by a visit to Bucharest's most famous confectioner, Capsa. He had been an apprentice to Boissier in Paris, where he learnt to make delicate pastries, crystallized fruits and chocolates. He offered French elegance and high quality goods until the Russo-Turkish war in 1854, when the Russian Army supply service, who knew a good thing when they tasted it, requisitioned his business. All went well until the day when drunken Cossacks stole all his stock and recipes and smashed his restaurant. Utterly ruined, he started afresh, teaching Bulgarians how to make a sticky jam out of rose petals, and made enough money to rebuild Capsa's in Bucharest. I remember it in 1939 making the most wonderful gateaux and chocolates which were sold in wooden boxes with dovetail corners. Secretly, I hoped that we might be related and able to guzzle Capsa chocolates for ever more. Mother was horrified at the suggestion that there could possibly be a family connection. I was delighted to see in 2003 that Capsa's had had a facelift and was still going strong after 150 years.

Between the world wars every street corner had a different smell and not all were pleasant. There were street stalls selling small black sausages smelling strongly of garlic, pierced with slivers of bamboo and dipped into spicy red sauce. Other stalls offered garlic bread and cups of steaming onion soup. Beneath the stall there was usually a bucket of greasy water in which the china cups were rinsed. Some vendors had trays hanging from their necks which were piled high with many kinds of Turkish Delight, sticky sweets stuffed with pistacho nuts and smothered in powdery sugar. Some carried cold water in tall wooden jugs and dished it out from a single metal cup on a chain clipped to the vendor's waist. Gypsy women gathered outside places like Capsa's, selling tight little bunches of delicately scented violets and lucky charms. Shop windows, using the new electric light, displayed the latest Paris fashions.

Young officers hovered around pretty girls like Lola sitting on benches beneath the plane trees watching their young charges. Some officers showed off like peacocks, driving smart carriages drawn by high-stepping ponies, others a troika at a canter behind three hairy-hoofed horses. The more affluent officers rode new-fangled bicycles. This was a hazardous pastime when wearing full dress uniform, boots, spurs and sword scabbards swinging near the wheels. High society also paraded in their carriages, seated behind coachmen wearing gorgeous velvet coats and top hats. They would all raise their hats if they passed the flamboyant Crown Princess Marie who drove a four-in-hand by herself and seemed to love every precious moment away from the irksome protocol of the Royal Palace and from her husband Prince Ferdinand. On fine evenings crowds thronged the pavements of the Strada Lipscani, tempted to step inside restaurants by strains of gypsy music and delicious smells of cooking.

In October 1902, my grandmother Alexandrina (Gui) Capsa at last received a dowry worth 4,500 lei from her parents, the Rallets. This was all recorded in spidery handwriting on a three-page 'Act of Donation', authenticated with nine rubber stamps and six signatures in black, violet and red ink. It listed paintings, lamps, clocks, carpets and a magnificent Bechstein piano, which was to have a great influence on my mother. There were also several ornately carved tables, sideboards and chairs which were removed to a museum in Ploesti by the Communists in 1948. My grandfather was posted to Galatz on the Danube where he lived in the Hotel Bristol and travelled by train to see his family whenever he could.

In 1906 mother, aged nine, was left a house at Doftana in the Carpathian foothills by her aunt, Anna Rallet, with the proviso that Colonel and Madame Capsa could live there for their lifetime.

An International Exhibition was held in Bucharest in 1906 to celebrate forty years of King Carol's reign and to show the world how much had been achieved since independence. The King made a rousing speech in Romanian, but it was practically unintelligible to his distinguished audience because of his guttural German accent. The King and Queen 'Carmen Sylva' came once, but Princess Marie came every night with her friends to dine in one of the open-air restaurants lit by Chinese paper lanterns hanging from the trees.

Well-stocked food shops and the easy living in Bucharest did not reflect the miserable life of the farmers. In desperation they sometimes ate mouldy maize and then suffered from a most unpleasant skin disease called pellagra. The Orthodox Church in Bucharest did its best to help. A silver coffin, which contained the remains of Dimitri, patron saint of Bucharest, was paraded through the streets. The sides of the coffin were embossed with pictures depicting the miracles of Saint Dimitri who was especially revered for his amazing ability to encourage rain to fall. If this holy peregrination failed to change the weather, then other saintly relics were paraded round the city. The priests, however, were no fools and had been known to delay the rain-making ceremonies until the skies were overcast.

The management of estates was left to middlemen, often Jewish, who, while financially astute, knew nothing about farming and the hazards of nature. The only thing that mattered was to balance the books. The harsh and insensitive treatment of the peasants resulted in a spontaneous revolt, initially against the middlemen. Attacks soon spread against all landlords.

The Peasant Uprising of 1907 spread so fast that the Austro-Hungarians were alarmed and massed their troops on the border of Transylvania. The Romanian Army Reserve was called up, 140,000 men deployed throughout the country and Bucharest cordoned off. In spite of many of them being sons of peasants, the soldiers killed thousands of peasants. The government received a nasty shock, due to its complacency in carrying out promised liberal reforms. New laws now recognized that even peasants were entitled to some rights. Curiously, the Peasant Uprising remained unrecorded until 1957 when the Communists claimed the event as their own and a postage stamp was issued depicting the event.

My grandfather was promoted to general in 1909 on his sixty-third birthday and given the plum posting of Commander of Constanta District, home base of the Black Sea Naval Squadron. His cousin, Matila Ghika, was stationed at Galatz and had made his name sailing four new torpedo boats built at the Thames Iron Works in Canning Town from London to the Black Sea. They were first naval vessels to cross Europe via the Rivers Rhine and Danube and were at one time drawn by horses 1,000 feet above sea level along the Ludwigs Kanal.

King Carol I's foreign policy may have appeared inconsistent, but this was due to an extraordinary secret treaty of friendship with Germany, which he made in 1888. He kept the single copy in his safe and only informed the Prime Minister some years later. This personal guarantee, repeatedly given by the King to support the interests of the Fatherland, was completely contrary to the anti-German feelings of his people.

In October, 1912, the Bulgarians, Greeks and Serbs declared war on Turkey and the Romanians were alarmed that Bulgaria might become the most powerful nation in the Balkans. There was intense anti-Bulgarian feeling and the citizens of Bucharest clamoured for war.

Ill-feeling erupted in May, 1913, when the Bulgarians turned against their former allies, the Greeks and Serbs. Such were Balkan politics that these countries were now supported by their late enemy, Turkey. The Romanians, except their monarch, worked themselves into a frenzy at the prospect of further expansion by Bulgaria and King Carol had no option but to order mobilization. There were scenes of wild excitement as reservists rushed back to their regiments.

On 10 July 500,000 Romanian soldiers crossed the Danube, but the war was just about over. The exhausted Bulgarians, unable to fight on three fronts, were disarmed and told to return to their villages. It was a hollow victory. Ferdinand of Bulgaria, who went to the peace talks in Bucharest, was humiliated and vowed vengeance. The Romanians, who had suffered few casualties, now had thousands of cholera victims. King Carol saved his reputation because he was able to claim that he was not a puppet of Austria and Germany, but it is unlikely anybody believed him.

In 1914 the Russian Imperial family decided to make a state visit on their royal yacht to Constanta. This was only the second ceremonial visit by a Head of State to Romania since Emperor Franz Joseph came in 1896. King Carol was delighted at the prospect. After weeks of planning my grandfather took his place alongside the Romanian royal family on the quayside. It was 13 June, 1914. The Russian ship, bedecked with flags, was eased into the harbour to the sound of a 101-gun salute from the elderly Romanian cruiser *Elizabeta*; the bands played and crowds cheered. It was an emotional start to a programme which went like clockwork and even included a moment for the Royal families to have a siesta after lunch. The one-day visit concluded with a magnificent banquet held in a tent decorated with flags and flowers. Unfortunately Crown Prince Carol, Ferdinand's son, and the Grand Duchess Olga, whom it was hoped he might one day marry, were not in the least bit attracted to each other and quite relieved when the time came for the Russian yacht to cast off and steam back to Odessa. It is sad to think that, had their feelings been otherwise, Olga might have been spared the awful fate which befell her family at the hands of the Bolsheviks in a cellar at Ekaterinburg. My grandfather, who had received the Order of St Michael of Romania, was now able to retire to his home overlooking the Doftana River.

Exactly two weeks after the Tsar's visit any hopes of peace in Europe were shattered by the assassination in Sarajevo of the heir to the Austro-Hungarian Empire. Amazingly, even though the penitent Serbs said they would accept almost every condition demanded by the bellicose Austrians, the Austrians still declared war. The Germans declared war on Russia on 2 August and then, with no warning, invaded Luxemburg and Belgium in order to catch the French unawares. Thus began the First World War, initially between the Allies (France, Britain, Belgium, Serbia and Russia) and the Central Powers (Germany, Austro-Hungary and Turkey).

The Germans demanded that King Carol should honour his secret treaty, but the Romanian public supported France and Britain. The arguments as to which side to support continued in Castle Peles at Sinaia between the German-born King Carol, Queen Elizabeth and Prince Ferdinand on one side and the British-born Princess Marie and Prime Minister Bratianu on the other. Encouraged by Italy's declaration of neutrality, whose example Romania often followed, the Crown Council decided to go against King Carol's strong recommendation to enter the war on Germany's side and chose to stay neutral. The King lost any credibility he may have had and there were rumours that he was about to abdicate. In the event the bitterly disappointed monarch turned his face to the wall and died quietly in his sleep in October, 1914. He had ruled as Prince and then King for a total of forty-eight years.

Chapter 3

BITTER BETRAYAL

There was a saying in the Balkans, 'Never trust a Romanian who wears his shirt tucked into his trousers,' the inference being that only peasants, who continued to wear national dress, were honest men. The new King, Ferdinand, was ill-equipped to face up to the devious politicians who surrounded him. Now, at the age of forty-nine, he lacked self-confidence and his mind drifted. Overshadowed by his attractive and extrovert Queen, he was an unhappy man. His only comfort may have been his mistresses, who included my Tante Ephrosine (actually my great aunt). These ladies were tolerated by Queen Marie who valued the freedom which allowed her to enjoy the company of attractive men like Barbo Stirbey.

At the start of the First World War both sides spent huge sums buying Romanian crops and oil in order to deny them to each other. Bucharest was full of people who speculated in commodities. As usual the peasants received no benefits. The Romanians were obsessed with the understandable wish to unite all Romanian-speaking people in Eastern Europe. There was never a question of Romanians going to war to help their friends; the aim was to decide what would bring with it the greatest gains. The dilemma was that the Romanians in Bessarabia were under Russian rule, fighting with the Allies, whilst those in Transylvania were under Hungarian rule, fighting with the Central Powers!

The Central Powers did not mind which side Romania supported as long as she entered the war. Either way German troops were going to occupy the country and open up communications with Turkey and Bulgaria. They would help themselves to the entire mineral and agricultural resources of Romania. Politicians chose to ignore the fact that the Army was hopelessly unprepared for war. My uncles, George and Cotan, both in the cavalry, had attended courses in French military schools. They were depressed at the total dependence on

German equipment. Not a single delivery of military equipment had reached Romania in the past three years. There were scarcely enough reserves of ammunition to sustain six weeks of war.

Two other uncles, Jean and Nicu, transferred to the newly formed Air Service in 1914, which was equipped with vintage French aircraft. Mother was photographed standing beside one of these fragile machines with her white Saluki hound. The young Capsa brothers no doubt told their father that, of twenty-eight divisions, thirteen were completely untrained and five did not possess a single machine gun. If the King and his advisors had been a little wiser they might well have decided to stay neutral a little longer. Sadly, it was all too much for my grandfather who died early in 1916. His open coffin was placed on an ornate hearse draped in black, drawn by a team of black oxen, because all horses had been requisitioned. I have not yet discovered where he was buried.

In the spring of 1916 the Allies insisted that Romania invade Transylvania. It was perhaps the only moment Romania could have made a significant impact on the war and got away with it. But she missed her chance. Romania informed the Allies that she would declare war on 27 August and requested that the promised Allied offensives begin immediately.

Russia moved 20,000 men into Romania instead of the 50,000 they had promised and these, amazingly, included a division of Serbs who had deserted from the Austrians. This was too much for the Bulgarians who were prepared to respect the Russians but loathed the Serbs. Seizing the chance to avenge the humiliation they had suffered in 1913, they declared war on Romania. The British attacks on the Somme failed, the French in Serbia never attacked as promised and, thanks to Russian duplicity, none of the arms promised by the Allies ever reached Romania. Nevertheless, the first few weeks were exhilarating for the Romanian soldiers, liberating their comrades in Transylvania. Unbeknown to them, the Austrians were only making a tactical withdrawal.

When war was declared it was a beautiful evening in Sinaia; the casino and the restaurants were full of people. As they watched the sun set behind spectacular jagged mountains they heard a deep rumble, like distant thunder coming from the north. Soon the mountain valleys began to reverberate with the sound of gunfire, which preceded the invasion of Transylvania. People rushed to pack up their villas. Crowds converged on the railway station where trains bringing soldiers to the front were soon filled with panic-stricken civilians. German air raids on the city terrified the populace. There were no air raid shelters and no anti-aircraft defences. Romanian pilots were no match for the Germans, experienced in battles over France. Using airfields in Bulgaria, the German pilots were able to make two sorties a day. Uncle Nicu Capsa was shot down flying one of the last fighters left to defend Bucharest. His name is on the splendid memorial to fallen airmen of 1916–18 on the highway to the airport. At night Zeppelins dropped many bombs, including seventy-two around the royal palace, killing a portrait painter. The British and the French assured the Romanians that there would only be ten divisions opposing them. There were no Allied supporting actions and after two weeks there were no less than thirty-eight divisions against the Romanians. Initially Romanian soldiers just managed to hold their own against overwhelming forces but they were unprepared. Their trenches were not deep enough. They were untrained in mountain warfare and had no artillery with a high enough trajectory to hit enemy targets on reverse slopes.

Prince Matila Ghika, mother's cousin, was sent as a liaison officer to the Russian Admiral de Verraillon whose ships provided naval gunfire support to the hard-pressed Romanian, Serb and Russian troops retiring northwards. Matila witnessed the final moments when the big guns of the old Russian battleship *Rostislav* destroyed Constanta just as the Bulgarians entered the city in a torrential thunderstorm. He then distinguished himself under fire in his motor torpedo boat, escorting vital supply barges to safety in the Danube Delta.

The Romanians retreated behind the Seret River and into Moldavia. Bucharest was again seriously threatened. For a short time the British flew air cover from Macedonia. Sir John Norton-Griffiths, a British MP, set about destroying the stocks of oil. His only equipment seemed to be a sledgehammer and a box of matches. The Government was advised to leave immediately for Jassy, the ancient capital of Moldavia. Queen Marie, who had distinguished herself working in military hospitals, was put on a special train with her staff, mountains of baggage and some foreign diplomats. The King, for all his imperfections, remained behind to retreat with his soldiers.

My mother, aged twenty, remembered the horizon black with smoke as she and thousands of refugees trudged past the Ploesti oil fields towards the mountains and the comparative safety of her house at Doftana.

The Central Powers now set about stripping Romania. Nothing was spared; even the rich black earth was taken in train loads back to Germany. The population of Jassy increased from 50,000 to over 200,000. A train carrying 700 wounded soldiers arrived from the front but only 60 were still alive. Typhus and cholera broke out, even among doctors and nurses, 200 of whom died. The mortality rate from amputation was high. That winter snow blocked roads, animals died of starvation and nothing could be transported anywhere. Queen Marie tried to put some spark into her lethargic husband and get him to visit his troops more often. Her son, Prince Carol, had fallen in love with Zizi Lambrino. The constitution imposed on Romania by the Great Powers stated that the royal family must never marry a Romanian. Prince Carol wrote renouncing the throne, deserted from his regiment and fled to Odessa, where he married Zizi, but before he could enjoy a honeymoon the royal train and the Queen's ADC arrived to collect him. His father sentenced him to three months' imprisonment in a monastery and annulled the marriage which was never announced.

On 12 August 1918 the Battle of Marasesti began. The army, which had been equipped and trained by the French, completely outfought the Germans. This brilliant success was acknowledged by the British Prime Minister, Lloyd George, who promised that he would not forget what Romania had done for the Allied cause. A week later the Russians on the Romanian flank mutinied. Thousands deserted and threatened the very existence of Romania. Cavalry had to plug the gap. Uncle Cotan, who had got himself a nice billet near Focsani and a lonely widow to keep him warm that bleak autumn, was horrified to be deployed along the River Prut.

For three months Romania fought the Russians. Then, abandoned by her friends and completely surrounded by hostile forces, she was forced in May 1918 to give up every bit of land she had gained and to being in debt to the Central Powers for ninety years, to forfeit oil-fields and railways, to cut down forests, dismantle factories and supply vast quantities of grain and livestock to Germany. She had lost almost as many young men as the British Empire (750,000). It was an awesome price to pay for the disastrous decision to go to war unprepared.

Queen Marie opposed total surrender and remained confident that the Allies would still win. Mother returned to Bucharest and enrolled as a nurse in the 'American Hospital'. Many of the wounded had fallen in the last desperate stand on the River Arges trying to save Bucharest. They were lucky to have survived the savagery of the Turkish infantry who bayoneted every living creature in their path. Then, a year late, the promised offensive by British, Serb, Greek and French troops began. The Bulgarians surrendered in September 1918; the Germans now offered Romania a revised treaty granting new borders. King Ferdinand ordered his ministers to play for time. The Austrians were the next to surrender. King Ferdinand, promising the peasants universal suffrage, mobilized the army and ordered the Germans to leave the country within twenty-four hours. The citizens could hardly believe it. For several days afterwards there was great hunger because the Germans had taken with them every scrap of food, every cooking utensil, every vehicle and cart. Then on 1 December 1918, after two years, the Royal Family returned to a memorable welcome. The King and Queen, both in uniform, rode down the Chaussée Kiseleff, accompanied by the French General Berthelot and preceded by Romanian and Allied troops. Micheline Capsa watched from Tante Ephrosine Ghika's house. It had been a close-run thing for Romania. I do not believe mother ever forgot those awful war years. Uncle Cotan, however, never found his widow again. Who knows, he mused? We might have founded a dynasty.

PART II
1920–1945

Chapter 4

SPRING WEDDINGS

In order to show that Bucharest was now back to normal King Ferdinand decided to revive the blessing of the River Dimbovitza. My mother joined the small crowd which followed the Metropolitan Bishop of the Orthodox Church and a cohort of bearded clergy with pink noses. Their dirty well-worn shoes showed beneath their black cassocks as they processed, reciting prayers and flicking holy water ahead of them. A ragged line of shivering soldiers stood on the river bank waiting for the Bishop to reach the centre of a bridge. A military band, which had been hastily re-formed after the war, played with gusto but little precision.

The Bishop waited patiently until the royal family had been ushered to their seats, five leather chairs placed on the bank opposite the soldiers. Then, with his arms outstretched, the Bishop blessed the turgid waters beside which Bucur the shepherd once pitched his tent. With a loud cry the Bishop cast a huge floral cross into the river. The soldiers hesitated for a moment, then jumped into the chilly waters and formed a line to intercept the floating cross. After they had helped each other out they laid the cross at the King's feet. He thanked his audience briefly and gave each sodden soldier a gold coin before climbing back into his carriage and hurrying home. The Bishop made his way back to the cathedral, his attendants carrying the somewhat bedraggled cross. Mother watched the ceremony wearing her father's old coat and was delighted to find a 100-lei gold coin caught in the pocket lining. She decided to take her friends to tea at Capsa's Restaurant.

The Royal Palace was one of the few buildings not looted by the Germans, perhaps as a mark of respect for the King's German ancestry. Citizens who had endured hunger and oppression were now listless and lacked the will to restore their damaged homes. Those who had the money to do so had fled to Moldavia. Now few could return because there was no transport. The retreating Germans did not leave a single serviceable railway engine behind. A few engines which had been patched up vibrated and wheezed along at a walking pace with clouds of steam seeping from every joint. The drivers made frequent stops in the countryside to allow the frozen passengers to climb down and forage for fuel to keep the firebox alight. The only seats were wooden slats and shivering passengers blocked the broken windows with blankets.

The River Danube was still frozen and blocked with sunken barges. The retreating armies had requisitioned thousands of horses to haul carts laden with loot. Oxen, which could have hauled carts, were slaughtered to feed the hungry. There was scarcely a motorcar left, except King Carol's blue Rolls Royce.

Not only was the nation at a standstill but there was a great shortage of manpower. Romania had lost almost as many men as the whole British Empire. There were weeping women in every village who needed a man to thatch the roof, dig a well or plough the land. Unlike the rest of the Allies, the Army could not be demobilized in 1918 because of the threat from Russia. The Romanians doubted whether the Allies would now honour their promises which had been such an important precondition to Romania's entering the war.

When the victorious Allies met in Paris in 1919 they showed so little interest in the Balkans that one might have assumed that they agreed with a remark once made by Bismarck: 'The whole of the Balkans are not worth the bones of a single Pomeranian Grenadier'. The Romanian spokesman, Ion Bratianu, was hopeless at explaining why new frontiers should include large groups of his kinsmen who had been living under foreign rule for centuries. Sadly, his arrogance and insistence that the Allies must now honour their promises upset the statesmen. Queen Marie, in despair at the mess he was making, was begged to come to Paris as soon as possible. She was already a heroine far beyond her own country and when she arrived in March, 1919, she was determined to let the world know just how much Romania had sacrificed so that the Allies might be victorious. She made a tremendous impact on the sceptical heads of state, who, because the Americans were in a hurry to sail home, eventually agreed to accept Romania's new frontiers.

Meanwhile, Béla Kun, a disciple of Lenin, installed a communist government in Hungary. The Allies sent observers who reported that

Béla Kun was quite harmless, but, just after they left, Béla Kun invaded the new country of Czechoslovakia and imposed a Communist government. He then invaded Transylvania. The diplomats in Paris still refused to allow the Romanians to intervene. Eventually they allowed the Romanians to retaliate, under command of Marshal Foch. A crushing defeat was inflicted on the Hungarians, but Romanian feelings, pent up for the past three years, gave way to an orgy of pillage worthy of Genghis Khan. Everything looted from Romania was recovered with interest, from railway engines to the last bottle of Tokay. Sadly, they went too far and this was bitterly resented by the Hungarians and the Allies, especially the Americans, who demanded that the Romanians withdraw. This they refused to do, unless the Hungarians recognized the Treaty of St Germain, which had granted Transylvania to Romania. The Allies actually imposed a blockade of Romania, which created more hardship until their withdrawal was completed in November, 1919.

With so much tension in the air, the conscript army could not be demobilized until 1921. There is little doubt that Romania's military actions delayed the spread of Communism into Eastern Europe for twenty years, but this setback to Lenin's ambitions did not deter him for one moment, because, by the end of 1924, Russian communists had seized eleven more republics, such as Armenia, Georgia and Mongolia.

Romania was now the fifth largest country in Europe and her population was starving. Appeals to her Allies for food resulted only in the Canadians sending three shiploads. The British and the French quite incredibly demanded commercial concessions in return for food, which Romania declined to give. Eventually the British released their military stocks of bully beef, biscuits and tea which had been left behind in Macedonia three years earlier. The French and the other Allies gave nothing. Faced with such a food shortage, it was decided to placate the peasants and the conscripts about to be demobilized by giving them land. All the big estates were reduced to a maximum of 600 acres, but they were allowed to keep their forests. This created a new landed middle-class peasant who felt that at least he now had a stake in his country's future.

Queen Marie reopened her country palace at Cotroceni, just outside Bucharest, where she invited many talented artists to perform. My mother remembered playing a white piano, which is still there, in a room full of stupendous flower arrangements. She treasured a signed photograph in a silver frame which the Queen had given her. From the age of eleven she had been encouraged to play the piano by George Enescu who sponsored her visit to Paris in 1919. On her return she gave recitals at the Royal Palace and in the Opera House which received acclaim in the newspapers: 'We were overwhelmed listening to her interpretation of the Andante by Schumann ... Mlle Capsa provided us yesterday, thanks to her remarkable talent, with moments of ineffable artistic joy.'

In 1920 she was invited to play at the Russian Embassy in Sofia. She wrote to her mother, 'I have met a Monsieur Siegrest who is Swiss, do please be nice to him', but then switched to her real target, 'Please, please, look out for Monsieur Pasinaro. He is *très sympatique*, owns lots of factories and has a capital of 400 million lira. Tell him I shall be back in ten days'. Sadly there is no record of what happened to any of these promising associations. In those days twenty-three was quite old still to be unmarried.

Crown Prince Carol, whose runaway marriage to Zizi Lambrino had been annulled by his father, was again causing consternation. He had already made a shop girl pregnant and now it was announced that Zizi was pregnant. The Crown Prince wished to resign from all his royal responsibilities. King Ferdinand, in an attempt to separate them, asked his son, who was stationed in Moldavia, to attend a parade in Bucharest. The Crown Prince said he could not attend because he had fallen off his horse. His father then decided to send him on a State Visit to the Far East, whereupon he shot himself through the leg, an act which drove his father to despair. When Prince Carol's regiment moved into Transylvania to fight Béla Kun's Hungarian invasion, he refused to go unless he was allowed to re-marry Zizi. Eventually he went, but wrote a letter of abdication to take effect after his return.

Everybody, including his brother officers, tried to dissuade the lovesick Prince from abdicating. Those trying desperately to protect the dynasty were much relieved when he finally agreed to give up Zizi, who gave birth to a son in January, 1920. She was given a pension and 5,000,000 francs paid into a Paris bank account. She and the baby were put on the Orient Express and removed from Romania. She was deeply upset that Prince Carol had not bothered to see his son before leaving on a voyage round the world.

28

With that crisis over, Queen Marie began the task of persuading her children to set a good example and marry the 'right' sort of person. In 1921 Prince Carol married Princess Helen of Greece, his sister, Princess Elizabeth, married the Crown Prince of Greece. One year later Carol's other sister, Princess Marie, married King Alexander of Yugoslavia. Thus three of the four Balkan nations acquired sovereigns from the same family.

There was so little in common between Prince Carol and his wife Helen that it is amazing a marriage ever took place. Yet in October, 1921, Prince Michael was born. Then, either to escape Carol's attentions or just on impulse, Princess Helen took the baby back to Greece to show her parents. She stayed four months, which was a fatal mistake, because by then, as was his wont, Prince Carol had already begun to look elsewhere for his pleasures.

The pattern of traditional village weddings remained unchanged until after the Second World War. As soon as a girl was old enough to marry, a single flower was painted on the outside wall of her home. Weddings usually took place between young people who lived in the same or neighbouring villages. However poor the families were, it was an occasion for feasting and dancing. Wedding guests walked barefoot to the bride's home and only then put on shoes which were often uncomfortable because they were worn so seldom. Everybody wore a dazzling array of embroidered blouses, aprons and waistcoats decorated with flowers and geometrical patterns. Married women wore coloured headscarves, each knotted differently, while unmarried girls wore flowers in their hair.

A wedding might last two or three days and, as was often the case, families were so poor that everybody contributed towards the cost. The bridegroom and his best man would gallop to the bride's home to claim her with lots of panache and a fiery speech. It was almost marriage by capture. She was carried out of the house and the groom demanded that she should serve the guests a farewell feast which had been prepared by the women of the village. They served this from large tureens outdoors beneath the lilac and apple blossom. There would be speeches, toasts in plum brandy (*tuica*) and gypsy fiddlers playing a lament (*doina*) because the bride was about to leave her home for ever, only to return if invited. Before leaving for the church the guests would hold hands and dance the *hora* (a traditional circle dance), while the groom and best man were helped on to their horses and galloped to the church to greet the arrival of the bride. She and her attendants either walked or rode in a spotlessly clean decorated cart, drawn by four white horses or six white oxen, followed by the guests, many of whom were again carrying their shoes.

The village priest, or '*popa*' would probably be the only person present at these occasions who had not yet enjoyed a glass of *tuica*. In my village, Doftana, there was a washerwoman called Vetta, who confessed to my mother that the *popa* had refused to marry her unless she appeared with a sober bridegroom. The *popa* only relented after she had taken him aside and pleaded, 'If I bring the bridegroom back to you sober, oh *popa*, it is highly unlikely that he will ever marry me!' The marriage service was concluded when the *popa* joined their hands together, placed crowns on their heads and pronounced them man and wife. He then removed the crowns and bound the couple together with white ribbon or even chains which the bridesmaids, in fits of giggles, swiftly removed. The dancing, singing and feasting would begin again, until the exhausted village and newly-wed couple were allowed to sleep. The next day in some villages youths would run down the street waving the sheet taken from the marriage bed which they had been given by the bride's mother. She made quite sure that, even if it meant killing a cockerel, the sheet bore a red bloodstain and thus proved it had been her daughter's first love.

Chapter 5

EARLY TRAVELS IN ROMANIA

As I have already said, I was born in 1925 and was brought up at Doftana, near Cimpina, in the foothills of the Carpathians. My grandfather, Mihai Capsa, a retired General, died there in 1916. His first wife had died, leaving five children. He then married my grandmother Alexandrine Rallet (Gui) in 1895. My mother was their only child. My English grandfather, George Redgrave, was an actor who took the stage name of Roy and married an actress, Ellen Maud Pratt, whose family lived at Littleham, near Exmouth in Devon. He left her and his children, Robin, Jack and Nellie, when he returned from the South Africa War in 1901. He lived for a short time with Esther Cooke, 'Ettie Carlisle', daughter of a circus owner. They had a son, Victor. A year or so later he went through a form of marriage in Scotland with one Margaret Scudamore, 'Daisy', an actress. They had a son Michael, who became a famous actor, was knighted and was the father of Vanessa, Corin and Lynn. But he deserted her too, to join another actress, 'Minnie' Titell Brune, in Australia, where he died in 1923.

My father, Robin Roy, was born in 1897. He joined the Royal Field Artillery in 1916 and was sent to Palestine to fight the Turks. After the war his stepfather, F. J. Nettlefold, helped him to start work in his oil company, Dacia Romana, in Romania. My father lived in a peasant house in Doftana near the oilfields. He married my mother in 1923 in the church of Saint Spiridon in Bucharest.

I spent a very happy childhood at Doftana, but the village is still remembered because of its dreadful prison; the first inmates included the leaders of the Peasants' Revolt in 1907. Political prisoners were forced to work in a nearby salt mine until the mine collapsed after an earthquake in 1914. It filled with water and became a very salty green swimming pool where my father had first met my mother. They had no common language except French. There was another earthquake on 10 November, 1940, which partly destroyed the prison, killing many prisoners, trapping them in their dark cells. I was blissfully ignorant of what went on inside (or for that matter anywhere else). I was brought up with my two sisters in comparative isolation at Doftana. In 1934, aged nine, on holiday from Lambrook School in England, I was allowed to accompany my parents on their travels.

Mother strode purposefully up to the guesthouse, whose owner had been waiting for her on a bench outside. 'The rooms are ready for you, madam,' she said, rising, 'please follow me.' She led us up a steep flight of stairs into a bedroom, threw open the green wooden shutters to let the afternoon sun come streaming in. The brass knobs on the bedstead positively glistened, the lace bedspread over a red duvet was crisp and clean. Nevertheless, Mother pulled back the covers and sniffed, 'How many people have slept in these sheets?' she asked. The landlady replied, 'Oh madam, just the new *popa* and two schoolmasters. Both appeared to be very clean, I assure you.'

'I will take the room if you change the sheets,' said Mother. This was probably my first great travel adventure other than the journey the previous year to England on the Orient Express. We were about to embark on a great expedition, drifting down the River Bistrita on a huge log raft. The trees had been felled on the slopes of Mount Pietrosu, stripped of their side branches and slid down steep runs to the fast-flowing river, where they formed a huge log jam. Skilled loggers had made two rafts, each of about twenty logs, which were lashed together at either end. They then placed newly sawn white planks on top in order to make a deck. A crude table and two benches were then constructed and fastened with 15-centimetre nails. The two rafts were joined to each other and were then loaded with enough provisions for ten people. These consisted of several flat loaves of unleavened bread, a huge circular cheese, a leg of smoked ham, two crates of grapes, several salami sausages, bottles of water, wine and Azuga beer. As if this was not going to be enough, my mother had brought a huge straw hamper packed with other, but in my young eyes quite unnecessary, supplies such as napkin rings, a cocktail shaker, toothpicks and marshmallows.

The raft was steered from the front by two men with huge oars, shaped like rudders, who balanced themselves on the slippery and constantly moving logs. When we had floated round a steep bend we suddenly found ourselves in a spectacular gorge. The two loggers shouted to each other above the roar of the water, strained at the oars and miraculously negotiated a route through the rapids and whirlpools. Every time we hit a submerged rock there was a great jolt and the food nearly slipped off the planks into the white water, as the logs bounced and slithered over the rocks. In the late afternoon the raft was rammed at the riverbank and secured to two trees. We were close to a small township called Brosteni. We disembarked and headed for the local guest house, along a dusty road with a pack of mongrels snapping at our heels, past flocks of geese and ducks wallowing in the foetid water of a drainage ditch.

For once not even my mother's obsession with cleanliness proved enough. She had inspected every inch of the bedroom and even searched the bedclothes for alien bugs. To do this she had perfected a secret weapon, a damp bar of Pear's soap, which she stroked over the sheets and examined every few moments to see if she had picked up any fleas or bugs. Then she checked to see if the four pewter bowls in which the bed legs stood had enough water to drown any unwelcome small visitors. Well-satisfied that the bed was now an impregnable sanctuary, she retired. Hours later there was an unbelievable noise coming from her room. She had been bitten, not once but many times. The electric light revealed a line of little insects climbing through the open window, up the wall and across the ceiling to the electric light flex which was suspended directly over the bed. Down they marched until they reached the bulb at which stage they let go and dropped onto the bed. Mother was hysterical.

There were other walks through the mountains when we followed coloured marks painted on trees or rock face. On one route we climbed up rough pine-branch ladders beneath and through a series of waterfalls, while the timid members of the party who did not want to get soaked were obliged to go the long way round. A camp site awaited us. I don't know who carried the tents there, let alone the sleeping bags. Mine was particularly heavy because it was made from two sheep's wool carpets stitched together. These proved to be much too hot. It was a joy to sit round a log fire cooking trout and kebab and to listen to amazing stories told by my uncle Cotan. Once, on a wolf-hunt, he had paused to guzzle some wild raspberries. Totally absorbed in his hunt for bigger and juicier fruit Cotan found himself looking eyeball to eyeball through the bush at a large brown bear who evidently also liked wild berries. Cotan had been discharged from the cavalry following an injury sustained when falling off his horse fleeing in panic from an angry husband. Once again what little courage he possessed had deserted him. He gave a loud yell, 'to frighten the bear,' and fled, leaving his musket behind. The bear was no doubt greatly astonished and wandered off to find another wild raspberry bush. Cotan returned cautiously to rescue his rifle which he then fired into the empty bush, just to show that he was still master of the situation.

We once drove down to the Danube where the current turned dozens of waterwheels. The peasants used them not only to grind maize but also to lift water into an ancient irrigation system and onto the fields. I found walking in these parts very boring, even with the possibility of an occasional distant glimpse of a Bulgarian soldier. Suddenly an immense black cloud appeared out of nowhere.

'There is going to be an almighty storm,' cried someone. 'Quick. Let's take cover on the veranda of that little house.'

We started to run just as one or two great raindrops began to fall. The picnic party reached shelter just as the heavens seemed to open. After fifteen minutes the peasant's house was surrounded by a sea of mud. To some of the ladies the little white privy at the bottom of the garden could well have been in Istanbul. The men gallantly offered to carry them through the mud. This was firmly declined by the wife of the United States ambassador, a lady from Texas, who approached the edge of the veranda. Arching her back and bending her knees, she gleefully cried, 'Mighty kind of you gentlemen, but I can shoot just as straight as any man on his two feet,' an accomplishment which I never forget and which, after some hesitation, she concluded, to much applause.

On another trip it was threshing time and outside every village there were little groups of peasants beating the corn with flails. Others, their backs to the breeze, were throwing corn and chaff into the air with wooden shovels, a method that had remained unchanged for centuries. I was to witness similar scenes in Tibet fifty years later. By chance my father was able to show me a 'modern' threshing machine on the same day, driven by a belt from a tractor. I was fascinated. Both methods, however, were being served from crude wooden carts, drawn by slow-moving oxen or buffalo, which were piled high with hand-tied sheaves of corn.

The peasants, I recall, were all wearing Romanian national dress. The men wore white smocks and white drainpipe trousers and the women were in embroidered skirts with open blouses, some of which carried a little delicate red silk embroidery. Very few peasants in those days owned more than one pair of shoes, if any at all. Guests at a celebration in a neighbouring village would normally walk barefoot and only put on their precious shoes for the last kilometre. Without shoes, it is amazing how they were able to work in the rough stubble, but wearing shoes so seldom was also painful. Some bound rags round their feet, others cut small strips of rubber tyre and bound them to their feet with rags. I remember seeing Russian soldiers in 1945 wrapping rags or ribbons round their feet.

On another occasion the gypsy camp beside the River Doftana below our house was in a high state of excitement. There had just been a wedding and broken pottery lay on the grass. It seems that, like a Jewish wedding during which the bridegroom smashes a glass to symbolize renouncing his former life, in this case the groom had chosen the bride's most precious piece of pottery to break. She was only a child and had probably been sold by her parents, who were now drinking the profit. She looked miserable and very frightened. My father took a silver pencil out of his pocket and gave it to her as a wedding present and made a small speech. She was pathetically grateful, but a few moments later her husband came and took the pencil from her. He then sold it to another drunken tzigane (gypsy) and put the money in his pocket. My father was furious, but could do nothing. Later, he bought the pencil back and was able to arrange for the girl to receive another small present. That night we could hear a noisy argument coming from the camp. The bridegroom was trying to attack the bride's father, saying that the girl was not a virgin, that he had been swindled, and anyway she kept complaining that he was hurting her. I do not know what the outcome was because my father hurried me away. It seems that there were no blood stains to indicate that the bride had been a virgin and he wanted his money back. I learnt, years later, that the bride's mother usually keeps a few drops of chicken blood handy to avoid such misunderstandings. Virginity was an important factor in ensuring a good price and children were sometimes married by the age of twelve, often having their first child soon after. I was never allowed to visit the gypsy camp alone because all sorts of terrible things happened there. When I pressed my Romanian grandmother to explain, she hesitated and then whispered, 'None of the tziganes ever wear underclothes.'

The Carpathian Mountains were a wonderful place in which to walk. A climb up through the dark forests led to a bright green grassy plateau, beneath towering rocky cliffs. It was then that the crisp air, the fantastic views and the excitement of never knowing when you might see a bear or a wolf made it an exhilarating and unforgettable experience. Sitting with my Uncle Cotan outside a shepherd's hut we looked down at the distant valley and a nearby sheepfold in which the shepherd kept a few chickens. Suddenly, from high up in the sky, a huge eagle plunged down and seized a hen in its talons. The shepherd rushed inside for his gun and we ran toward the pen, but it was too late. The eagle and the squawking fowl were high in the sky, heading for a nest in the cliffs. I said that I had never seen such a huge bird, whereupon the shepherd took me into his woodshed where a huge golden eagle was nailed to the timber. The smaller brown and white eagles attack chickens and lambs, whereas the golden eagles go for smaller animals, including snakes. This one had failed to get a good grip on a snake which managed in flight to entwine itself round the eagle's neck, forcing the bird to land, whereupon the shepherd killed them both.

I had grown up to accept the presence of good and evil spirits in a house. Once or twice a year the *popa* came up to the house with a magnificent cross hanging round his neck and a copper jug filled with holy water which he sprinkled from a brush made of twigs on the wall of every room to make sure the evil spirits stayed away. He was given a substantial donation to church funds and left his little brush to be split between the female staff who slept with it under their pillows in the belief that their dreams would one day come true.

In the mountains, however, tales of Dracula and vampires still existed and Cotan loved to tell a tale. He had entered a cottage and was almost overcome by a strong smell of garlic, bunches of which hung round the living room; a huge bunch of wild thistle was tied to a beam above the front door. It was normal to have a cross in every home, but this house had at least ten. He discovered that a few weeks earlier a man had committed suicide in the village, and, although the

36

elders of the village wished to plunge a stake through his heart before burying him, the priest refused. Needless to say, the man had returned as a vampire. His first victim was a white turkey, his second a suckling pig, and only two days before a young girl had been struck by a mysterious wasting disease. Then two little scratches were discovered on her neck, possibly vampire's teeth. The village wanted to dig up the suicide's body, cut off the head and stuff his mouth full of garlic. The priest refused, so the villagers covered the grave in thorns and thistles so that the shroud would be caught as it tried to leave the grave. Some people even wished to kill the girl. She was terrified because none of her family would come near her. She tied her foot to the bed so that all could see that she never left the room at night. Cotan had a young doctor friend who realized that she had probably scratched her neck entering her room on a bunch of thistles hanging above the doorway. He treated the scratch with ointment and it soon vanished, but the prejudices and fears of the villagers remained.

In the mid-1930s in a Carpathian village, an old woman, long suspected of being a witch, threatened that when she died she would be back to haunt them. The terrified peasants seized her body and determined to make sure she stayed in her grave. They cut off her head and, as was the custom, stuffed her mouth with garlic. A massive stake was driven through her chest then, to make sure that everybody would hear her coming, they nailed horseshoes to her feet!

Uncle Cotan told me many stories about the Danube Delta, whose inhabitants included Turks and Russians. The Russians were called Lipovans, a religious sect who had been persecuted in the days of the Tzars and were probably made even less welcome by the Communists. At one time all the drivers of horsedrawn cabs in Galatz were Lipovan or Skopzi. Some were voluntary eunuchs. These eunuchs were described by Cotan as being overweight and flabby, with heavy jowls. He explained that they wore long black coats and their voices were perfectly normal. It seems that it is only if you are castrated while still a boy that your voice goes up! The sect was founded in about 1780 by a peasant called Selivanov who persuaded his followers that he was Christ come to earth a second time. They must have coexisted with that other strange sect, the Dukhobors, who were pacifists, refusing to pay tax on buttons. They fled to

Cyprus in 1898, their trip paid for by Quakers in England. A year later they moved on to western Canada where, until the invention of the zip fastener, they must have felt the cold.

Cotan's stories never failed to excite or entertain. He described how when he reached a river in the Danube Delta region there was no bridge or ferry to be seen. He stood with his companion on the bank and shouted for the ferryman to come and collect him. Nothing happened, but a small boy pointed to a black buffalo in the water. 'There is your ferry,' he said. 'Put your clothes on top of his head and fasten them to his horns with the shirt sleeves. Then hang onto his tail. It is only 100 metres. You will soon be there.' While he got dry on the other side and retrieved his clothes, Cotan talked to a fisherman on the veranda of his cottage. There were nets, ropes and fish traps, strings of fish drying in the breeze and a pair of oars and a pole for his boat. Every now and again a gentle sound came from the strings of a mandolin being played somewhere inside.

'Who is playing with the instrument?' asked Cotan.

'There is nobody there,' replied the fisherman. But just then another chord was heard, as if somebody was drawing a bow of a violin gently over the strings of the mandolin. The fisherman went inside, took one look, grabbed a weapon and killed a water snake that was trying to get inside the sound box of the mandolin. If I had been older I might have asked Cotan to explain to me the politics, corruption and sex in Romania which he knew so much about, but, as usual, I left it too late.

My last great travel adventure in 1939 was on the Orient Express, returning to school in England. The International Sleeping Car Company had been bought by George Nagelmachers in 1887. The railway only went as far as Vienna where my grandfather, Captain Mihai Capsa, returning from a military course in France, had to transfer to the Danube Steamship Company. Ten years later the line was extended to Constantinople and Bucharest. By 1906 the Orient Express had acquired quite a reputation. Every coach displayed an impressive list of European capitals. Of course not every stop was listed and small towns took great pride in having been selected as worthy of a stop. One such town was Cimpina, 5 kilometres from our home at Doftana, where the train stopped for two minutes. Grandfather, who was the provincial Governor, had insisted that the train stopped there before making its final run to Bucharest through fields of maize and sunflowers past clusters of oil derricks.

The First World War put a temporary stop to the Orient Express, but by 1921 the service had become increasingly popular. There were by now all sorts of customs and immigration controls. This was taken as a challenge by my mother who smuggled a bolt of taxable white satin by sleeping on it right under the officials' eyes. She brought some silver packed at the bottom of a kitbag in which she had packed boxes of talcum powder with loose lids. The unfortunate official plunged his arm into the kitbag, only to have his uniform covered in white powder. He looked no further.

I calculated that I spent up to three weeks a year on that train between 1934 and 1939. I therefore had that much less holiday than other boys. The journey ceased being an adventure. There were lots of black uniforms, searches for Jews and a wreath on the platform at Vienna station with a black ribbon in memory of Austrian Chancellor Dollfus, who was assassinated by the Nazis.

In September 1939 the Orient Express and Nord Express routes to the Channel ports were closed. I was eventually sent back to England on the Simplon Express. This unpleasant journey took seven days just to Paris, which we reached during an air-raid alarm. Soon afterwards the Simplon also ceased to run, when Italy invaded the South of France. For a brief moment in 1942/43, when the whole of Europe was occupied by Axis forces, an 'ersatz' Orient Express ran from Paris to Bucharest.

After the war, when travel was restricted because of the 'Iron Curtain' across Europe and because of competition from the airlines, the Orient Express as I knew it never ran again. However, in 1976, on the 100th anniversary of the Wagon Lit Company, I was commander of the British Sector of Berlin. Among my tenuous links with West Germany was the British Military Train. This used to leave Charlottenburg Station in Berlin every day for Brunswick in West Germany. Among its coaches there was a blue Wagon Lit dining car with a Union Jack and the badge of the Royal Corps of Transport painted boldly on its side. The doors were all locked on departure. The train had a British military guard, a radio transmitter and dry rations in case the train was held up by the Russians, who were the only people with whom we could discuss anything to do with the train.

When I travelled on the train on the 100th anniversary I did as my grandfather might have done in 1976. I walked to the dining car and ordered a bottle of Pommard and gazed at the proud steam engines which were then still in service in East Germany. I reflected on the extraordinary history of those blue coaches and the thousands of people who escaped to freedom on them in time to avoid the Nazis.

Chapter 6

THE FLOTSAM OF WAR

I was sent back to school in England in October, 1939. My father escaped being arrested by the Iron Guard in Romania in January, 1941. He rejoined the army, aged forty-three, and was sent to Ethiopia and Somaliland with the French Foreign Legion. He then went to Persia, Syria, Palestine, Morocco, Egypt and Italy. My mother was able to leave Bucharest with the British Embassy staff for Egypt in February, 1941. She made the difficult decision to leave my sisters, Mary Maud, aged thirteen, and Ioana, aged eleven, behind under German occupation with my grandmother. Eventually they too got out, thanks to the endeavours of the Swiss ambassador in 1942, and were reunited with my mother in Cairo. In 1943 all civilians were evacuated from Egypt to South Africa, where they remained for two years.

I left Sherborne school in 1943 and, in order to avoid conscription into the coal mines as a 'Bevin Boy', I volunteered to be a regular trooper in the Blues and signed on for seven years with the colours and five with the reserve. This, as recounted in *Balkan Blue*, un-expectedly lasted for thirty-seven years!

After a gap of six years the whole family, less Gui, my Romanian grandmother, was briefly reunited in England for just three days on 30 August, 1945. I then had to return to regimental duty in Germany.

In 1988 I opened a green gasmask case which had lain inside my father's battered tin trunk for at least forty years. It contained identity discs and a curious collection of personal documents: letters, ration cards, movement orders, microfilmed Forces Air Letter forms and the messy carbon copy of an unfinished four-page news letter. It had been typewritten in French by my mother, probably in Cairo, in April, 1945. She was trying to bring her readers up to date with what had happened to their mutual friends since 1940 and she obviously

41

gleaned little scraps of intelligence from everyone who visited the British Embassy where she worked as an accounts clerk, the only job she could find.

They had all been members of a carefree cosmopolitan society which flourished in Bucharest right up until Romania entered the war in 1941. It had been a traumatic experience. Their lives and the Romania they had known were now in turmoil and the only certainty was that nothing would ever be quite the same again.

The letter begins: 'Elizabeth has grown so fat it is unbelievable! George and Mihai Brancovan were both killed in flying accidents with the Romanian Air Force. Ioana Leonte's son was killed on the Russian front at Stalingrad. Ionel Popescu, Marioara's husband, that ardent pro-Nazi, has suddenly become an Anglo/Russophile and, it is said, has even offered his house to the British Military Mission. Jean and Nadejde Poulieff have also been able to switch their loyalties. Indeed many of the Iron Guard have now become ardent Communists. Bazu has married his beautiful Jewess, a Madame Curvinstein, or some such name! Max Auschnitt gave a huge wedding reception afterwards, but neither Alice nor Maruca would attend.'

'Peter Perrott', the letter continues, 'became a lieutenant in the Coldstream Guards and was killed by a sniper in Italy. Count Romedio Thun von Hohenstein became a Hauptmann (captain) in a German Cavalry regiment. He was in charge of a squadron of Cossack deserters. He always believed he was a Czechoslovak citizen and had no wish to join the German army. He was wounded in Yugoslavia and is now a prisoner of the British in Austria.

'Bobby Walters went back to America and is now in the US Marine Corps. Donald Walters, his brother, may become a Buddhist monk and is now in California. Hambique was mobilized into the French Artillery somewhere in the Alps where he fought against the Italians but has since disappeared. Poor Yvonne Burileanu's son has been a prisoner in Russia since 1942.'

Never one for wasting time on small talk, Mother determinedly questioned everyone passing through Cairo for news of her friends. She must have sifted through all the letters she had received, and carefully preserved, throughout her wanderings since she left Romania in 1941. Although the extracts she selected are often quite unrelated, they nevertheless reflect the shattering result of a calamity which befell a civilized group of people who suddenly realized that, whether they wanted it or not, their respective countries were from then on at war with each other.

Her letter continues: 'Lisette Parvulescu has left her husband for a Spaniard whom she followed all the way to Spain, but only then did she discover that he was fed up with her. Her husband married a certain Melle Botej whom it appears was even more flighty than Lisette. Sanda Ghika, Leatitza's daughter, has divorced Radu by whom she has an enchanting four-year-old daughter, and has now married Nicu Grigorcea, a charming young man, it seems.'

A severe earthquake and Allied bombing attacks on the oil refineries at Ploesti had evidently caused widespread destruction.

My mother continues: 'Leatitza's house does not exist anymore, neither is there much left of Bonaparte Park. That lovely house belonging to Lascar has been destroyed and so have the homes of Paf Grigoresu and Eny Koslinsky. Their vineyards were badly damaged at the same time and are now completely neglected. Paf, incidentally, has married someone with a very doubtful reputation.'

Many of the British who worked in Romania returned as soon as the Germans pulled out, but they were immediately regarded as a menace by the New Order which the Russians, already in Bucharest, wished to create in Eastern Europe. They were all told to leave the country, including my father, who was there in uniform in a military capacity. He was flown back to Bari in Italy within twenty-four hours of arrival.

My mother then starts to list their names: 'Donald Hitt, Eisinger, Galpin, Gwyn Elias, John Warry, Ted Masterman, Bill Young and many others you don't know are now back in Romania. Joe Slomniki joined the Royal Engineers and was sent to Tehran to look after Polish refugees. He, too, is now in Romania. He has seen Irene who has turned grey and works terribly hard. Elise has spent the last two years in Istanbul and has been advised by her family in Bucharest not to go back.

'Old Count Blome is still in a sanatorium in Brasov. His house in Voila was badly damaged by the earthquake. Jo and Christian have moved back to Prague. It is said the Nazis have put their son Kiki aged sixteen in prison.'

The rollcall of what had happened to her friends continues: 'Cance is now a Lieutenant Colonel. Poirault, that charming Frenchman, now has two children. Fifi Dupont has married a very rich cultured Jew from Alexandria. He is thirty years old and on the whole a much

43

better choice than Maurice, but he still plays around and she is not very happy. His family have disowned him and she dare not tell her family that he is Jewish.'

Of course, what all these exiles wanted to know was what life was like in Bucharest after four years of war. The only comparison mother could make was based on her typical pre-war shopping basket: 'The cost of living is quite astronomical. Can you believe it, a hat from Olympia's costs 50,000 lei, something which calls itself a dress 25,000. Lunch at the Athene Palace [where I was born] costs between 7,000 and 10,000. A kilo of caviar 100,000 and a pair of shoes 50,000. A workman in the Ford factory gets 60,000 lei, while the Director of the Telephone Company only gets 75,000, as you see an unfair proportion.'

She then lists all her friends who had died: 'Marcelle Catargi died the very moment the Armistice was agreed. She had been madly in love at the time with one of the Hohenzollerns, Chouche Ghika, who was killed in the American air raid. Didine Cantacuzene died in the same way. Nevertheless, many American airmen were looked after by our friends. Tom Masterman died in England last year of a brain haemorrhage and his wife died a few months later of cancer. Helen Slomniki has been in England for the past three months; like me she spent two years in South Africa. Vera Hitt has become an officer in the Wrens, which means she is with the Navy.'

At last she touched on her own family, beginning with her brother, a cavalry general: 'George was too old to be sent to the front, just as well, because his regiments of Rosiori were almost all killed at Stalingrad. He is not well. The Communists have moved into his house on the Calea Victorei. Maman is well and living in a small flat in town. Her house was flattened by bombs and the earthquake. Doftana, our old family home, is still intact, but I very much doubt we shall ever be able to live there again. My Aunt, Ephrosine Ghika, died in 1941.'

'Roy will be twenty in September. He is now a Lieutenant in the land of the windmills. His address is 1st Household Cavalry Regiment, British Liberation Army.' It was this reference to me serving in Holland that helped fix the date of the letter. She goes on to describe my father's movements: 'I have hardly seen Robin since we left Bucharest four years ago. The Army have already sent him to Syria, Persia, Eritrea, back into the desert and then to Casablanca. He is now in Italy waiting to go somewhere in the Balkans.'

44

There is a final flurry of information before the letter ends, just as abruptly as it began, describing the brutal change to collective farming. 'All the land and buildings have been taken over by the Communists except for 50 hectares and the sleeping accommodation. Livestock and agricultural implements have been distributed to the peasants. The Flondors, Grigoreas and others up there have been left with absolutely nothing. Prussy Caranfil passed through here a week ago to join her husband in England. Percy Clark, who was tortured by those filthy Iron Guardists, has recovered and is now a Court Martial judge in the Army. Pussy Calimaki has married a saxophone player in a night club band somewhere or other.'

For all those dispersed exiles, who at least were still alive after the war, there was a general feeling that now, at last, things would get better, even if it was not exactly like it was in the past. Little did they realize that Romania was about to become a People's Popular Republic and that the dismal dogmas and dreary doctrines of Socialism would, barely a year later, completely eradicate what little remained of the quality of life they had known in Bucharest. Imprisonment, forfeiture of their possessions, denial of education for their children, reduced rations and restrictions on travel were to become the new way of life. Only the lucky ones would be able to escape or be expelled.

Nevertheless, how could anybody forget the heady atmosphere, the gypsy music, the excitement and sensual pleasure of having once lived in Bucharest? Yet the background of political unrest, of corruption which delayed entry into the European Economic Community, and of the plight of the peasants, continues to this day. Things may be getting better, but the pragmatic belief that such problems are unavoidable and should be accepted as perfectly normal sadly still prevails.

As I delved deeper into the books and papers which filled the battered tin trunk, I learnt much more about Romanian history. It is sad that the golden age of Romanian development, 1920–1940, should have been marred by an abysmal lack of responsible leadership. The needs of the people were seldom fulfilled. As I folded the flimsy carbon copy of my mother's newsletter and returned it to the trunk, together with gas mask, mess tins and army pay book (3 shillings a day), I wondered what my grandchildren will think of it all when they go through the trunk many years hence.

PART III
1946–1965

Chapter 7

THE WENDISCH *WACHMEISTER*

1947, Wesendorf, Lower Saxony, Germany
When the Second World War ended the Russians were our glorious allies, but friendship soon became suspicion when we realized that they were never going to give up the occupied countries of Eastern Europe. The Cold War was about to begin.

Wachmeister Waneke's autocycle refused to start; it seldom did; however hard he kicked the starter, it always needed more encouragement. He cursed his luck because today he was expected to attend an important meeting at the old air base just outside the village of Wesendorf, where a squadron of British armoured cars was stationed. He pushed his inert machine along the three planks which bridged the storm ditch between his house and the road. He set the controls very carefully, primed the carburettor and then began to run, pushing his machine over the uneven cobbles. The moment he let out the clutch the little engine burst into life with a rush. He sprang onto the saddle, wobbling dangerously as he waved at the *Gasthaus* keeper, who chose to ignore him.

The *Wachmeister* had not been much of a soldier himself. Although he had been trained as a tank driver, he was deemed unsuitable for a panzer regiment. The reason could have been because he was Wendisch and not a pure Saxon German. The Wends are a tribe of Slav origin who still speak their own distinct dialect and for centuries have inhabited Mecklenburg and the eastern part of the old Kingdom of Hanover. He had developed a hernia and been posted to the railway control staff in Oradea in Romania, where he was able to spend a relatively untroubled war until the great retreat from Russia in 1944–45. Russian T34 tanks had halted for a moment while they waited for their infantry to clear a path through the Carpathian Mountains and break through towards Budapest and Vienna. To his

49

horror Corporal Waneke was ordered to form part of an improvised rearguard and delay the Russian advance from a hastily prepared position east of the railway station. As luck would have it, a group of nurses arrived and at the last moment the gallant corporal was detailed to escort them on a train through Hungary and back to Germany. The journey took many days and ended after an intense bombing attack near Göttingen. Waneke and the nurses fled from the train and hid in the home of one of the nurses. Waneke surrendered to the Americans just as the war ended on 7 May, 1945.

After the war he applied to join the police and was given an enormous questionnaire called a *Fragenbogen* to complete. This was scrutinized by officials of the Allied Military Government to make sure it did not reveal if he had any connections with the Nazis, which was pointless since every young person had been obliged to join the Hitler Youth. However, on the strength of his undistinguished career he was considered to be sound material for the new police force. His immediate superiors had no illusions regarding the calibre of the man they had recruited and sent him to Wesendorf, a remote corner of Kreis Gifhorn, which bordered the Russian zone. On this spring morning he decided that riding over the cobbles seemed more uncomfortable than ever, so he switched to the summer dirt track which ran alongside and was much preferred by horse-drawn vehicles. The cherry trees which lined the road were soon going to blossom. He had high hopes that he might one day be allowed to rent a few trees and, who knows, he might then be able to make his own Kirsch liqueur, which his wife Trudi liked so much.

When the little motorcycle spluttered into camp bearing a portly figure in a green uniform, Trooper Bellingham, the Intelligence Office clerk and an old Etonian, sighed, 'Oh dear it's our good friend the *Wachmeister* again, Sir. I wonder what terrible things our troopers have been up to this time in the village.' There had been a trail of minor destruction every Saturday night after the *Gasthaus* closed its doors, which was beginning to irritate the farmers whose homesteads lay alongside the road back to camp. I went out to greet him and the *Wachmeister* clicked his heels together and saluted.

'What is the trouble Herr Waneke? You seem to be worried,' I asked as we walked to my office and sat down beneath a huge map showing the Demarcation Line between the British- and Russian-occupied Zones.

With a dramatic flourish he drew a document from his briefcase: 'I have been instructed to set up a special committee with your help Herr Hauptmann. It should be most interesting. A local Venereal Disease Watch Committee, which should include your doctor and Dr Zeiss from Gifhorn. In this way we will eventually know which ladies, who, as you once said, should "be taken off the road" and cleaned up.'

'How on earth,' I asked, 'are we supposed to know which girls not to allow to the camp dances now?'

'Ah,' said Waneke. 'First we wait until one of your men makes a mistake and becomes ill, then I shall put the girl's name on my special file index. I now have 200 cards.' Then he dropped his voice to a whisper, 'On some cards I have already entered the girl's name, in pencil, mark you.'

'That does not seem to help my men,' I protested. 'Why can we not warn them before they pick up the girls or for that matter why can we not catch the drunks before they start to break windows?'

'Alas, everybody would like me to do that,' sighed Waneke. 'They all think I am a useless policeman. But what is the point if the land-lord of the *Gasthaus* refuses to give evidence? He is making so much money that he can afford to pay for new window panes in his house every week.' I agreed with him. We had tried identity parades on Sunday mornings, which included, as in that classic film *Casablanca*, 'rounding up all the usual suspects,' with no success whatsoever.

'There is another serious matter,' the *Wachmeister* went on. 'The Russians at Oebisfelde at the border crossing point have now begun to make difficulties for anyone they catch who works for the British. There are many people in this village who visit their relatives in the East and who believe that, with your help, I can stop the Russians behaving so badly. But I tell them I fought on the Eastern Front. I know what terrible people these Mongol soldiers can be. They stop at nothing.'

Waneke closed his eyes evocatively, hoping that nobody would realize that he had never actually seen a Mongolian soldier, let alone fired a shot in anger.

'All right,' I said. 'Don't worry about the VD Watch Committee. I'll help you to get it started. Now go over to the Civil Labour Office and find out all about these people who have had problems with the

Russians. Where did they cross? Where were they taken to and what sort of questions were they asked?'

I paused and, as an afterthought, added 'Would you like to come with me next time I drive along the border? Then we should be able to see the problem for ourselves.'

The *Wachmeister*'s face paled for a moment at the thought of coming face to face with a Russian soldier, but then he considered the immense prestige he would gain if an armoured car came to collect him from his home. 'I would be happy to accompany you, Herr Hauptmann.' He clicked his heels smartly, saluted and turned about, only to trip over my Irish setter which had decided to lie down just behind him. Having salvaged his dignity, he must have prayed that his autocycle would start first kick. It did and he set off in a cloud of blue smoke for the Civil Labour Office, situated behind an aircraft hangar, to collect a few facts before going home.

The Demarcation Line had been established in June, 1945, when the Allies were obliged, by agreements reached at Yalta and Potsdam with the Russians, to pull back from positions they had occupied along the River Elbe at the end of the war. The actual frontier now followed the old provincial boundaries between Nieder Saxony in the West and the provinces of Schwerin and Magdeburg in the East. On the ground the line was practically invisible. Sometimes it followed the course of a stream, the edge of a forest and an occasional marker stone, inscribed KP or KH, which I took to be Kingdom of Prussia or Hanover. Where the frontier crossed a road or a farm track the Russians had dug a ditch or felled a tree and dug foxholes in which their unfortunate soldiers stood day and night. The main official crossing point was at Helmstedt where the Hanover to Berlin autobahn, the railway and canal all crossed into the Russian Zone. But there was still another crossing at Oebisfelde where every day a queue of travellers waited for hours to pass through a Russian control post beside a small bridge over the Mitteland canal.

The *Wachmeister* and I stood on a low bank overlooking the crossing point and watched a red and white barrier being lowered by two Russian sentries after a tractor-load of potatoes had been searched and allowed through. The first house on the left over the bridge was a guardroom, which all passengers entered to have their *Ausweis* document (passport) stamped. Occasionally a dejected figure could be seen being escorted into a building painted yellow, outside which Russian military vehicles were parked.

'That is the old school house,' whispered Waneke. 'It is their headquarters and where interrogations take place. They stripsearch people, even women,' he added meaningfully. 'Once they find the pink Pass Card which you issue to all employees, then the questions begin. Even if they say they only work in your kitchens, Senior Captain Govorov, with four stars on his shoulder boards, makes many difficulties. They miss their trains. He even takes their food parcels. Before him there was a good man who understood the problems we Germans have; at any rate, provided he was given a packet of cigarettes or a bar of chocolate.'

We continued our patrol and made a note of other possible places to cross which avoided Russian standing patrols. As the weeks went by the difficulties increased. There were many villagers whose relatives lived only a few kilometres away, but were already in the Russian Zone and living in another world. Naturally these travellers tried to bring them tea or coffee, but for weeks Senior Captain Govorov continued to exert a baleful influence on their lives. The villagers were in a dilemma; they needed the work which the British provided, but did not wish to be victimized by the Russians. The unhappy *Wachmeister* had a miserable time, because the villagers reckoned he ought to persuade the British to make their Russian Allies behave more reasonably. He also was none too popular with the Quartermaster when he suggested that a solution might be to withdraw all civil labour from the camp and let the army do its own housekeeping.

Perhaps the last straw came when Trudi, his wife, who originally came from Rathenow near Berlin, decided to visit her grandmother before all travel was stopped, an event she felt sure was going to happen sooner or later. She had been one of the nurses whom he escorted back to Germany and had then hidden him in her home in the Harz Mountains.

He missed her cooking and took his meals in a quiet corner of the *Gasthaus* while she was away. Three weeks later she returned with a hair-raising description of her adventures, including a skirt-raising body-search by a German-speaking woman who wore black rubber gloves. However much she loved her grandmother, she was not going to endure all that again. But Trudi was also an observant girl who had noticed a civilian mechanic working on the Russian trucks in the school yard at Oebisfelde.

'It was Boris,' she said excitedly, 'that Bulgarian who worked with you in Oradea and who you smuggled onto our train. I could recognize him anywhere, that big black moustache, his olive skin and that little white speck in his left eye. Oh yes, it was Boris. The Russian captain was angry with him and kicked over a tin full of screws from an engine he was mending.'

Somehow, she was sure that with the help of the King of England and Boris, we were now going to be able to turn the tables on her tormentor Captain Govorov.

'Let me have a talk with the British. I have an idea,' said her husband. In fact he had no idea what to do! He was at his wit's end how to re-establish his authority in the village, especially in the eyes of the Burgomaster, who had been considering his record with a jaundiced eye.

A few days later his autocycle developed an electrical fault as he rode into the camp and he was obliged to push it to my office. I asked a soldier to take it round to the workshops and invited the *Wachmeister* to the officers' mess to wait until the machine had been repaired. Downstairs in the washroom his eyes lit up when he saw the vomitorium, complete with two chrome handles, a padded headrest and a large flush button.

'So you still have some good parties here, Herr Hauptmann?' he asked.

'No,' I replied a little stuffily. 'It has not been used since the Luftwaffe were here.' The *Wachmeister* looked around the room. He had never seen pictures and military prints on the walls of a gents' washroom before. He studied one frame in particular, containing five postcards depicting Russian Horse Guards of the old Imperial Army inscribed 'With Easter greetings to their British Comrades 1916'.

We went upstairs to the anteroom where I ordered a glass of beer for the *Wachmeister*. It arrived in a silver tankard with a glass bottom on which was depicted a man hanging from a gibbet and the words 'Ye last droppe'. He stared at the bottom and said slowly, almost in a whisper, 'We can get rid of Senior Captain Govorov, almost like that.'

'What on earth do you mean?' I asked in a hushed voice, even though the room was empty.

'You must send him a postcard with good wishes from his British Comrades, just as we saw on the picture downstairs. All mail from the West to the East is censored. I do not expect that Govorov ever receives a private letter. Everybody will be interested, especially if it is a picture of English soldiers. Anyway it will soon be Easter, so it is a good time to send it.'

'How are we going to know if the letter is delivered and what happens afterwards?' I asked, my interest fully aroused.

'Well, you see, there is this man Boris,' and he went on to explain all about the Bulgarian mechanic. 'I will establish contact with him and then ask him for information from time to time. Maybe in the end we will have to help him. I am sure you will be prepared to do so, especially if he gives you inside knowledge about your Russian neighbours.'

'But why should one Easter Greeting card remove Govorov?' I asked.

'Because, Herr Hauptmann,' he replied, 'you will then send another card and another, and in the end he will be unable to prove that he is not in regular contact with the British. Your messages will always thank him for his letters which you will never receive, but nevertheless they will contain some true scrap of information about life in his company which my friend Boris will supply.' He finished his mug of beer.

'What a brilliant idea! Don't tell anyone, because if my colonel ever gets to hear about it I shall be in trouble. Let me telephone to find out if your machine has been repaired.' I returned with an old Christmas card showing a moonlight cavalry charge in Egypt in the late nineteenth century. I wrote the message in a bold hand and addressed the envelope 'Senior Captain Govorov, 276 Motor Rifle Battalion, The Old School House, Oebisfelde'. I handed the envelope to the *Wachmeister* to put in the post box. Both of us were slightly stunned by what we might have started.

The next few weeks passed quietly enough; no one believed the *Wachmeister* when he hinted darkly that there might be some important changes in the regiment on the border before the summer was over and that travellers would suffer less harassment. The Burgomaster promised Waneke that, if this was true, he could have the crop of every fruit tree between the village and the British camp. Waneke prayed that he might soon receive news from Boris. A few days later a local dachshund dealer brought a note from his contact on the border. It was written in Wendisch and unintelligible even to the courier. The postcard had evidently arrived and been seen by all in the Russian Headquarters building, leaving everyone very puzzled. The next day the Political Kommissar made his routine visit. Govorov showed him the card and the Kommissar had it taken away.

I called at the *Wachmeister*'s house to be given the news. Trudi, who had started a charm offensive, fetched coffee and apple strudel and then blew softly into my ear, sending shivers through my body.

'What secret games are you two clever boys planning now? I am sure that I can guess,' she said as she fled into the kitchen. Our next card depicted Lancers skewering mutineers in India. I thanked Govorov for his message. 'What a pity,' I wrote, 'that the Political Kommissar has taken the card', and I enclosed another for his private collection. Thus the saga continued.

Waneke was worried that he did not have enough reliable sources who could contact Boris and thus keep up the pressure on Govorov. He decided to visit an old friend of his father who lived just over the border in the village of Wendischbrome, an original settlement of the Wends. It took him an hour to reach the village of Zichere-Bochwitz, split into two by the new demarcation line. In the distance he could see the church in Wendischbrome and in between the two was the farm which he intended to visit. On the roof of a large barn there was a cartwheel, on top of which a massive nest had been built by storks. Two young birds were being fed by their parents. He rode in under a carved wooden arch and was given a warm welcome. They had a son who worked on the railway and whose steam-engine often crossed the border at Oebisfelde where it handed its load to another loco-motive before returning to the West. He handed them two cartons of cigarettes out of my special funds and they were happy to try to establish a link with Boris.

On his return journey the *Wachmeister* took a short cut through the heath where, to his amazement, he noticed, tucked away amongst the silver birches and pines, a huge British tank. There was no sign of the crew or of any tents, but he did recall that there had been man-oeuvres in the area before the 'battle' had moved northwards towards Luneburg. It seems that, unknown to the *Wachmeister*, the crew had suffered acute food poisoning, the radio had failed and, bored with waiting for help, they had abandoned the tank and moved into a convenient *Gasthaus* a mile or so away.

Our hero climbed on to the Comet tank, for that is what it was, and discovered that the turret lids were locked, but not the driver's. He lowered himself into the driver's seat and examined the controls which were not all that different to the Panzer Mark IV on which he had done his basic training. There was a gear stick, two track steering levers, a clutch and a master switch. He turned it and a little red light came on; he pushed a button and to his surprise the engine burst into life. He was just about to see if he could move the tank when he remembered his autocycle leaning against the side. He climbed out and lifted his machine onto the engine cover and climbed back into the driver's seat. He engaged gear, cautiously let out the clutch and the tank lurched forward. He got it onto the track and set course for Wesendorf. After travelling a few miles his self-confidence and enthusiasm knew no bounds and soon he was scudding along, scattering chickens, stampeding herds and startling villagers. He roared into the British camp which had never been designed to take tanks, right up to the headquarters building, where, unsure how to stop the monster, he turned off the master switch and the tank rolled to a stop just inches from the Padre's car. The Colonel, the Adjutant, the Regimental Corporal Major and sundry dogs of all sizes rushed out to greet him. For some reason the cool English phlegm which he had grown to admire seemed to have deserted them. There was much alarm and much barking. He climbed out of his seat to stand on the mudguard over the track. Then, seeing the Colonel, clicked his heels and saluted smartly, '*Wachmeister* Waneke reporting. *Ich habe einer grosse Panzer gefunden!*' (I have found a large tank). Waneke's stock went up.

Meanwhile, in Oebisfelde things were beginning to look bleak for poor Senior Captain Govorov. Our last postcard had thanked him for a present which he had never sent and commiserated with him that the new BTR 40 armoured car had broken down the first time it was used on the frontier (information supplied by Boris). Govorov now sensed he was being watched closely and in order to show his deep commitment to the Party he became even more brutal to any frontier-crossers who appeared before him. The final blow came with a letter containing a Havana cigar and a reference to the Commanding General's Zis staff car which had failed to start at the end of his inspection visit. Govorov was removed that very afternoon, never to return. Unfortunately the only people present when the car failed to start other than the General's party were Govorov and Boris. The NKVD or military police were naturally anxious to interview Boris, whose day off it was. A timely warning from a fellow worker prompted him to flee immediately. Boris hid until dark, then walked away from the frontier until he reached the Mitteland Canal, where he hid in the cargo of a barge and escaped to the West.

A few days later the telephone rang. It was the *Wachmeister*.

'He is here in my office with some fantastic news.'

'Who on earth are you taking about?' I asked.

'It is Boris. Govorov has gone to the salt mines in Siberia.'

'I will be with you in twenty minutes,' I said and rushed to the mess to buy a bottle of cherry brandy, which I knew he liked, and a box of chocolates for Trudi.

Boris was given temporary employment in the camp fire brigade, until we could get rid of him. The *Wachmeister* had advised me, 'You must not trust that man even though he has been useful this time.'

The grilling of our employees seemed to have eased and the *Wachmeister* got his fruit trees. The villagers were proud of their policeman who could still drive a tank, who had fought the Russians to a standstill and who now had outwitted the tormentor of innocent travellers from their village. The landlord of the *Gasthaus* actually telephoned for help and two drunks causing damage were arrested. It was generally felt by the Burgomaster and the local authorities that Waneke needed something more than his little autocycle to go about his duties. Three weeks later a smart dark green Police Volkswagen 'Beetle' was delivered to his house.

On the first day he was to use the car, which had a silver police crest on its door, Waneke dressed slowly, savouring the occasion. He was flattered that his ability had at last been recognized. He was bursting with pride as he looked out of the window at the group of small boys admiring his car and bent down to give his boots another rub with a duster. Then, as he buttoned up his tunic, he heard the radio news broadcast with growing disbelief. The Russians had blocked all routes to West Berlin, every single crossing road, rail and canal, but not yet air routes. He called to Trudi.

'So it was all for nothing. Did you hear that?'

Well at least he'd got a new car out of it. He would have plenty to talk about at the VD Watch Committee in Gifhorn later that morning. He put on his cap, took a quick look at himself in the mirror, picked up his briefcase containing the new card index of vagrant girls and walked over the ditch to his car. He was conscious that all eyes were on him as he unlocked the door and got inside. He put the ignition key in the starter and turned it, but not a sound came from the engine. He tried twice more with no better result, before he buried his head in his arms and wept.

Chapter 8

THE HONEY BAG FLING

1955, Northwest Territories, Canada
There was a polar bear sitting on the roof of the officers' mess of the Canadian Arctic Warfare School at Fort Churchill on the Hudson Bay. We were lining up for breakfast when the Paymaster spotted it. He urged us to stand absolutely still and slipped inside the hut, only to reappear with a loaf of bread he had grabbed from the toast-making machine. He offered it to the bear with some remark such as, 'Hey Buster, try this,' and tossed the loaf to one side. The bear slid down the roof and moved off to seek the loaf while we dashed inside. I do not remember much about that course, which was supposed to be an indoctrination for NATO and Commonwealth officers who were studying at the Canadian Army Staff College in Kingston, Ontario.

We were taken on night marches in strong winds wearing snow-shoes. This was like wearing huge tennis rackets strapped to our boots with long wooden tails which sent stinging snow into the eyes of the man behind. There was a drill for almost everything we had to do. For instance to pee or crap at −30 degrees, 'Concentrate on what you are trying to do, take a deep breath, unzip trousers, locate shrivelled member, shoot straight, have paper bag ready. If you miss it will soon freeze solid, crumble into dust and contaminate the camp area.' Inuit, we were told, were less fussy, used a corner of an igloo or an annex to the igloo and put the huskies in to clean up when they moved camp.

I first met Henry Ross when the Royal Canadian Mounted Police took part in the Coronation procession in London in 1953. We kept in touch for many years. He was responsible for creating my keen interest in the Arctic, its wildlife and its inhabitants.

It was over twenty years since Royal Canadian Mounted Policeman Henry Ross first took a team of huskies high up into the interior of

Baffin Island to search for two missing Eskimo, now known as Inuit. They were perhaps the first victims of the failure of technology in the High Arctic. They died from cold after their new snow machine broke. The 'skidoo' is a snow vehicle powered by a two-stroke engine which drives a wide rubber track. The driver sits astride the engine and steers with a handle-bar, turning a short pair of skis. Originally designed as a pleasure vehicle during the long winters in Southern Ontario, it was not suitable for extreme weather conditions and heavy workloads in the Arctic.

The two men travelled fast to check on a line of traps. It was a beautiful morning and in a couple of hours they covered what would have taken a dog team the best part of a day to cover. An hour or so later the vibration caused a tiny screw to fall out of the carburettor and only then did they realize that they had travelled too far and too light. They had no spare parts, very little food and not even a snow knife with which to cut a snow house. They started to walk back. Corporal Ross found them next morning, frozen to death only 3 miles from the settlement.

Ever since the early Inuit trained a wolf cub to wear harness and draw a sled hundreds of years ago, dogs have been a vital part of Inuit life. Stories about huskies known as 'Quiminik' are legendary. They have an incredible sense of direction. They can guide a man lost in an Arctic 'white out' or blizzard safely back to his home. They are able to sense that beneath the snow ahead there is a crevasse or that just behind the next snow dune there is a polar bear. Their keen sense of smell has been known to lead a hunter, searching for seals on a frozen sea, to turn inland towards a herd of caribou which are just out of sight. Huskies have a remarkable sense of hearing and have been known to warn a settlement of the arrival of visitors with long-drawn-out howls up to two hours before they arrived. As a pack they are very dangerous indeed, having been known to kill children who come too close, and woe betide anyone who falls down in their path when they are in full cry. Corporal Ross always treated his dog team with great caution; he knew a constable's wife who had been seriously mauled by a pack. The travels of Staff Sergeant Jolly RCMP and his dog team in 1925/1926 did much to establish Canadian sovereignty over islands such as Ellesmere, Baffin and Devon. This was at a time when the United States had not yet acknowledged Canadian rights in the area.

61

In summer, when there is no work for husky dogs, they are allowed to roam and live by scavenging. They hunt lemmings and crunch mussels and shrimps, tear at roots and vegetation; indeed, they will eat anything except the liver of wolves and polar bear, which contain a high concentration of vitamin A and are very poisonous. Any traveller making camp always has to remember to place his snow-shoes, sled harness and leather trap lines well out of reach of his dog team before falling asleep. A tragedy struck a family who were crossing Baffin Island. They were caught by a sudden thaw one night while they slept. The snow wall, on top of which they had stowed their kit and a kayak, melted. The hungry dog pack destroyed everything before they awoke to the danger. With no harness to drag the sleds and no trap lines to hunt with, they calmly resigned themselves to death; only one survived.

Corporal Ross cannot stand the din of high-revving skidoo engines, often without silencers. He hates the way teenagers hop onto a machine as soon as their fathers return from a hunting trip and drive wildly through the settlement. The Inuit now has the mobility which no longer requires him to build a temporary shelter, like an igloo, because he gets round his trap lines very much more quickly. This has led to killing more game than they need. The young have to be reminded that keeping a herd of caribou at the canter for twenty minutes greatly increases the amount of calories they use and rapidly reduces the amount of grazing available for the herd.

There has been a dramatic reduction in the number of huskies, who for centuries have provided endurance, strength and companionship. The skidoo can only provide speed. You cannot cuddle up to a machine to keep warm, or eat it if you starve and use the pelt to keep warm. Dogs have stamina, whereas a skidoo cannot run on an empty fuel-tank. However, things have begun to change after a few deaths in the wild. The Inuit are obliged to carry spares and survival kit. They must never travel in less than pairs. The best arrangement Ross has seen was an Inuit sitting on a bright yellow skidoo drawing a sled on which his husky team was sitting, their heads up, noses into the wind, having a lovely ride.

When, as a young constable, he first came to the Arctic he was responsible for hundreds of square miles of the North-West Territories. Like all isolated RCMP officers, he was regarded as a father figure, almost a God. He represented every aspect of Government control, which faceless authorities in Ottawa, hundreds of miles away, hoped to exert over their nomadic citizens, the Inuit. He ran the Post Office, albeit with mail deliveries only once or twice a year; he issued game licences, paid pensions, dished out medicines and organized search parties. He represented the Law, white man's Law, to people who have had their own unique code of conduct for generations.

He has not dealt with any major crime in ten years, but he does know of a Corporal at Chesterfield Inlet who arrested a murderer. An Inuit had killed his wife and his mother-in law; they had nagged him incessantly. Being shut up in an igloo with them all winter may have driven him to think that there was no other way to stop the carping. Certainly his tribe condoned the action and the Corporal, when he investigated the affair, agreed pragmatically that the Arctic being what it is, the murder was inevitable. He dutifully informed Ottawa by radio, asking permission to handle the matter himself. Unexpectedly Ottawa decided to set an example with a trial.

A judge and jury were duly gathered together and flown to Fort Churchill where they spent a night before continuing their expensive flight northwards. The trial took place in the RCMP office, where there were not enough chairs. The bewildered Inuit pleaded guilty right away. However, the problem remained as to what sentence should be awarded. Traditionally, no Inuit has ever been executed and any obvious alternative such as life imprisonment would have delighted the man, who would never again have to go hunting, or build shelters, or carry kayaks or indeed fight the cold. The judge asked the Corporal what would cause this man the greatest possible inconvenience? The answer, clean out the RCMP hut for two hours a day for the next two years, a sentence the Corporal would have awarded anyway and thus saved a costly trial. The Inuit was left wondering what on earth all the fuss had been about.

Corporal Ross returned to be an instructor at the Depot in Regina and then, after three years, volunteered to finish his service in the Far North. He was appalled at the changes that had taken place in the Inuit communities. The effect of the white man's kindness and his concern for the Inuit had been so misguided that it filled him with shame. Well-meaning civil servants, teachers and nurses had arrived in the Arctic to administer the Inuit, to dish out welfare, to educate them, to introduce them to junk foods, plastic, polythene and paper containers. They brought gifts, not gold, frankincense and myrrh, but booze, venereal disease and third-rate television shows. This surfeit of tender loving care from a white government in distant Ottawa had begun to remove any incentive to work or respect for their ancient culture. Corporal Ross ceased to consider his role either important or rewarding; he might just as well be working in a deprived corner of Toronto.

Most settlements are within sight of the sea, at any rate in summer. In winter, with the sea frozen, it is difficult to tell where the shore lies. During those few weeks when the waters are free of ice an entire year's supplies arrive in ships and barges. These are unloaded into bright red landing craft and run onto rocky beaches. Thousands of drums of oil, food and clothing for the Hudson Bay Store and the personal household belongings of Government officials and families, like that of Corporal Ross, are dumped on the shore. There are prefabricated sections of identical houses, in which everyone, including the Inuit, are expected to live. What is disturbing is the total lack of thought that has gone into the design of these dwellings. They are fine for a milder climate 1,500 miles further south with picture windows on four sides and doors on two, but they are ill-suited for the Arctic, where each window causes twelve times more fuel to burn than a plain insulated section of wall. In winter most of these windows are covered up, whereas in summer the bright sun remains horizontal all day, so curtains have to stay drawn to keep out the dazzle. Little thought, either, has been given to the prevailing wind when laying out the settlement; houses are erected parallel to power lines and for the first time given a number to be painted on the door in bold figures.

Then, after a year, the track began to crumble, so it was decided to move the houses to firmer ground. It soon became obvious that it was impossible to persuade all the Inuit to dismantle and re-erect their house on a set date. The resulting new line of houses was not in numerical order. The young Government Administrator was determined to renumber the houses in an orderly fashion, but the Inuit had become attached to their original house numbers. After all, they never had a number on an igloo or a tent; this was surely part of their new status and white man's life style. They refused point blank to be regimented any more and appealed to Corporal Ross who lost no time in drilling some common sense into the Administrator. The jumble of house numbers remains to be remarked upon by visitors: 'How curious and confusing'. Confusing for whom, thought Ross, as he set about boarding up his windows before the winter.

Every summer the Inuit move out of their homes and set up hunting camps miles away. Ross always has difficulty persuading those left behind to clean up the mountains of rubbish around the empty houses revealed by the melting snow. Air charter flights now bring in tourists who cause him more headaches by losing their possessions. They often do not wear enough clothing, unaware that even in summer it can turn cold. There are also angling regulations to be strictly observed. The livelihood of the local Inuit depends on not allowing more than two Arctic char to be caught by one tourist. Ross has to make sure they do not hunt endangered species such as Atlantic walrus, blue humpback whales, polar bears or musk ox, whose killing has been prohibited since 1917. He also has to make sure that the boats hired by tourists are equipped with survival gear, maps and provisions. Finally, he warns them of the dangers of sailing too close to those huge, beautiful blue icebergs, ice which can smash through a steel hull or topple onto a vessel.

In the High Arctic there is permafrost; the earth stays frozen solid to over 1,000 feet deep. During the short summer only the top few inches ever thaw, so houses have to be built on legs, albeit short ones, so that a layer of cold air prevents the soil from being melted by the heat of the house. When this happens a house will gradually sink into a lake of its own making; prefabricated sections pull apart, currents of freezing air become cabbages of ice as they meet the warm moist atmosphere. Even picture hooks, which pierce the insulation, collect tiny icicles.

The provision of fresh water needs careful management. In most settlements it is pumped out of the nearest lake and delivered by water truck to those houses displaying a coloured card in a window, indicating that they have run out. When local supplies begin to look dirty the alternative is to visit a distant lake, load the sleds with blocks of ice and stack them outside each house. In time the corners are covered with yellow stalactites as more and more dogs cock their legs on the ice stack. Hence the local adage, 'Don't lick the yellow snow, sonny'.

Snow in the Arctic is much denser than the powdery snow found further south and far less has to be gathered to make water when camping away from the settlement. The problem does not end with gathering drinking water. How do you get rid of it? It will never flow away. It is impossible to dig a cesspit in the permafrost; there is no seepage; once the pit is full it overflows. So shower and dishwater pour out beneath the house. Those built on a rise are lucky; dirty water flows away before freezing. Those houses not so fortunate have a skating rink on their doorstep until a spring thaw reveals the uneaten pasta and plate scrapings after a long winter.

There is an expensive solution to this problem called the Utilidor, which is a heated duct on stilts linking every house. Inside are the hot and cold water pipes, as well as heated sewage, which flows to a point outside. This key to modern living was first installed in a new town, Inuvik, near the mouth of the Mackenzie River. About 2,000 whites moved into the town to share this southern comfort, but it is not certain that the Inuit and Indians were delighted.

In spite of the fact that the RCMP have been alerted to look out for bits of Russian space rockets, white man still has difficulty overcoming the simple problem that permafrost imposes on the disposal of sewage. The great symbol of living in the High Arctic is the 'honey bag'. This is a plastic bag inside a bucket, with a lid, placed in every shower room. The additional humidity this causes may be beneficial to sinus sufferers and certainly encourages the sale of air wicks and fragrant sprays at the Hudson Bay Store. Woe betide those who overfill their 'honey bags', leaving insufficient plastic to tie round the neck. Bags are dumped outside, where they soon freeze and are collected with rubbish and dumped a mile or two away. Visitors looking out of aircraft windows on a mild summer day might be excused for thinking that a yellow cliff contains a rare mineral strata.

When I met Ross again, now a sergeant, he was much disturbed by the deteriorating relations between native Inuit and white immigrants. When he first came to the Arctic the handful of whites had been traders, missionaries and policemen like himself. They had all tried to understand and adapt to life in the North; there was, after all, nothing else to do. They were able to form close friendships with some of the Inuit. Now there are many more whites, who bring their families and their interests with them. They are able to communicate daily with the South, and, apart from 'honey bags', live much the same sort of life as they have always done.

The white man no longer travels with the Inuit and does not need their help to stay alive as much as before. There is no longer any common meeting ground; there seems to be a loss of mutual respect for each other and a great social gulf seems about to develop. The whites have become patronizing and superior, while the Inuit become angry and hostile. Although education, health care and social services are provided and appreciated, they resent the rigid and insensitive way it is done. For instance they cannot understand why older children are sent away from home to attend school in the south. Why are sick relatives flown to distant hospitals where they cannot be visited? They much resent close family groups being broken up in this way and blame the Government Administrator.

This bleak state of affairs coincided with the breakdown of the vehicle which collected the 'honey bags'. All equipment breaks down at some time in the Arctic or cannot move because of terrible weather. The 'honey bags' then begin to pile up around the house. The plastic splits, the snow hides the bag until springtime, when all is revealed. People will do anything to get rid of their bags and the Administrator found his home besieged by an ever-increasing cascade of frozen bags. They would come flying through the night air or roll off speeding skidoos onto his front porch. The Administrator's children, back for their Christmas holidays, entered into the spirit of things and returned the bags with interest. Both sides complained to Sergeant Ross at the outrage of being hit by these bulky missiles. He listened quietly, told them he would give his verdict next day and meanwhile insisted on a ceasefire.

Sergeant Ross went round to see his old friend, the manager of the Hudson Bay Store, and together they rummaged round the stock room. Next day heads of families were assembled in the nursery school. Ross put the blame entirely on the broken machine and, in order to avoid similar problems, each household was given plastic bags in one of six colours. For the next two months bags were also to be tagged with house numbers. Houses within tossing distance were given different colours. On the principle of set a thief to catch a thief, he chose the occasion to announce that the RCMP would recruit Inuit Auxiliary Constables.

His decision was widely regarded as timely and sensible. As they dispersed, he reminded them about the Carnival next April which marked the end of permanent winter darkness. It was an occasion for traditional contests, snow-house building, tug of war, fishing through the ice, harpoon throwing, ice sculptures and dog-team contests. Sergeant Ross now proposed a new sport which he could see was already popular with everyone; a 'honey bag' tossing contest with rules similar to those of Olympic hammer throwing.

Thus it was that peace and good will was restored and the most popular event at the Carnival became the frozen 'honey bag' fling. This was won in its first year by none other than a certain Henry Ross.

Chapter 9

THE *GARDE CHAMPÊTRE*

1961, Crespières, France
I was posted to Supreme Headquarters, Allied Powers Europe, near Versailles, where my wife and I were lucky to rent a farmhouse in an unspoilt village to the west of Paris.

Madame Berthe was nearly always late for her daily task, that of ringing the church bell at a quarter to eight for Mass. Not only was she breathless but she was also flushed with excitement at the importance of her news.

She paused for a moment beside me to gasp, '*Monsieur, monsieur*, the *Garde champêtre* [village policeman] will be wearing his *képi*. They say he is going to direct the traffic in the middle of the village and that the President of France himself will be passing through.' She hurried on and I entered the *boulangèrie* where the baker's wife was handing out baguettes as if she was reloading a quick-firing anti-tank gun. In the queue was my friend, Monsieur Blanc, a retired 'fire-eater and sword-swallower', but he preferred to be known as an artist, albeit a circus artist. He turned towards me and said gravely, 'I hope that there will be a lot more police around to protect our President in these dangerous times than just poor old Henri with his *képi* and his whistle.'

Crespières was a small agricultural village 30 kilometres west of Paris, sufficiently remote not to have become a dormitory for city commuters. My five-year-old son went to the village school wearing a *tablier* (smock) with a satchel on his back. All his written work was initially done on a slate. At the end of term we were presented with his photograph seated at a desk with a carefully written message '*Moi, je n'aime pas l'école*': I hate school.

There were several kinds of civil police in France, as well as mobile brigades of the *gendarmerie* throughout the country and in the Army,

69

where they act as military police and use a wide range of military equipment, including light tanks and armoured cars. There was also the para-military *Constabularie Regionale de Sécurité* (CRS) who are specially trained to deal with riots and terrorism. They protected the President in the face of a real threat, at that time from the demoralized conscript army in Algeria. Finally, unsung and seldom praised, there was a lonely guardian of the peace in rural villages, the *Garde champêtre*. He received little training, had no equipment and seldom appeared to have any uniform apart from his cap, or *képi*. His duties seemed to be restricted to settling grazing disputes and adding a touch of dignity to local civic ceremonies.

It was universally accepted in the village that the *Garde champêtre* only wore his *képi* if the occasion was one of considerable importance. I had last seen him in full regalia, which included the award of the Croix de Guerre, at the Remembrance Day ceremony in the village square to which I had been invited, provided I wore my uniform, thus giving the occasion an international flair. Not only did he have the distinction of carrying the Tricolor, but he had to repeat the words '*Mort pour la Patrie*' after every name which the schoolmaster read off the War Memorial.

There were forty-seven names and poor Henri, now in his seventies, found it a lengthy and thirsty business. Throughout the Mayor's oration that followed, and then the schoolchildren's rendering of *La Marseillaise*, his flag drooped lower and lower, whilst his eyes kept wandering towards the bistro, *L'Auberge qui Chante*, where the civic traditional vin d'honneur was soon to follow.

Henri was a tall, distinguished-looking man. Many people observed that, when he was wearing his *képi*, he resembled President Charles de Gaulle himself. The only other people in the village with any sort of official headgear were the four voluntary firemen (*pompiers*) who wore 1911 fire helmets and looked very self-conscious in ill-fitting blue jackets with red facings. They were the mayor's private army and much in demand at weddings.

Henri had a sad lugubrious face and a slightly vague expression that gave little indication of his strength of character and courage. He was much respected for his worldly knowledge and for his distinguished military record. In the First World War he had fought in the Dardenelles and marched with the French Expeditionary Forces through Macedonia as far as Banat in Romania. In the Second World

War he had played an important role in the local Resistance against the occupying German Army and carried out particularly daring acts of sabotage on the railway between Paris and Rouen. He had once visited Italy and seen the leaning tower of Pisa, which made a marked impression on him; '*elle penche bien*,' he would say, indicating the angle with his hands. For the last twenty years he had never left the village.

The last time that he tried his hand at traffic control was during a Paris Motor Club Rally whose route passed through the village. It had ended in disaster. A miscalculation in the timings resulted in the first cars arriving before he had put on his *képi*, let alone taken up his position at the crossroads. This enabled a couple of drunks to direct every third car or so down a cul-de-sac into a waterlogged meadow, which ensured a memorable Saturday afternoon's entertainment for the villagers. Today he was taking no chances and arrived twenty minutes before the President was due to pass through. Henri took up a key position opposite the *charcuterie*, whose owner greeted him from behind a counter covered in steaks, pigs' trotters and blue hydrangeas.

The *Garde champêtre* had firm ideas about '*le traffic control*'. There was to be no question of letting traffic flow until the last moment; the only effective control was to stop it moving at all. He was going to invite drivers to park on the square outside the school and direct them to visit the bistro while they waited, where he expected that his old friend Monsieur Bertholet would benefit from the occasion.

The crowd of women who usually gathered round the water pump in the square every morning sent their children off to find out what was happening. The newspaper van, a noisy yellow baby Citroën, pulled up outside the *tabac*, whose proprietor hastened to collect a small bundle of newspapers. In no time full details of the President's intended visit to a nearby agricultural college were being read aloud, followed by a list of plastic bomb explosions in the city the previous night. The full significance of the *Garde champêtre*'s role began to dawn on the villagers; they nodded their heads and began to jostle for positions from which they could watch the presidential cavalcade pass.

Just then two very aged and noisy biplanes from a nearby flying club flew overhead.

'Ah, what did I tell you,' said Madame Giraud. 'They must surely be looking out for ambuscades.'

Her son was doing his military service on a nearby airfield at Villacoublay, so she spoke with some authority. A red diesel tractor towing a trailer piled high with steaming manure was halted by a magnificent gesture from Henri and directed to park on the square. The pink-faced labourers gladly switched off their snorting machine, asked a few questions and hurried into the bar. Several cars followed and parked neatly on the square. There were still about ten minutes to go when a huge lorry with a number plate from the Vosges, somewhere near the Rhine, charged into sight and reluctantly hissed to a halt with its radiator vibrating against the *Garde champêtre*'s back. Its hairy, muscular occupants, wearing grubby vests and green braces, lowered the windows and shouted at Henri, 'Come on, Grandpère; we have not got all day to waste in this manure-covered village.'

The situation was explained to them somewhat tersely by the *Garde champêtre*, who realized that he now commanded quite an audience. The driver and his mate shouted that they had already been diverted twice and that they were not going to move again. Indeed, they were adamant and suggested that if he did not move aside they would assist him. Quite suddenly there was a whiff of war in the air. The butcher was joined by his wife behind the *tête de veau* and the blue hydrangeas. More people gathered in doorways, upstairs windows opened and the retired sword-swallower grasped his walking stick a little tighter. As the tension grew a great silence fell on the village. The village postman arrived, parked his bicycle against a tree and was about to deliver something to Henri when he stepped back into the small crowd outside the bistro. At any moment the first of the President's convoy of Citroëns might sweep round the corner. Anyway, principles were at stake. There could well be an accident and the village receive bad publicity. Could not these barbarians realize that this was a very special occasion because, after all, Henri was wearing his *képi*?

Just then a veritable fusillade of shots could be heard from the direction of the main road outside the village. Then there were more shots, a few shutters closed discreetly, the two 'foreigners' involuntarily showed some uncertainty and their arguments ceased. Like his President, who seemed to savour each moment of crisis, the *Garde champêtre* rose to the occasion with great dignity and pointed imperiously to the square. The lorry from the Vosges engaged reverse gear and, with bad feeling, parked on the square.

'It is only the partridge shoot,' said Henri to the butcher. 'You can see they have never heard a shotgun before, let alone a machine gun!'

At that moment the postman detached himself from the crowd and walked across to shake Henri warmly by the hand.

'You were magnificent,' he whispered, 'but they telephoned a moment ago to say that the President's route has been changed and he will not be passing through the village. I would have told you sooner, but I just had to see you put those barbarians in their proper place.'

The *Garde champêtre* shrugged his shoulders and moved to the edge of the street where he took out a battered tin of tobacco and rolled himself a slender cigarette. He refused an invitation from the circus artist to have a pastis in the bistro with a shake of his head. Then he turned to walk slowly home through deserted lanes, a lonely figure with his *képi* tucked under his arm.

The office of *Garde champêtre* was once also that of town crier who would complete each announcement with the words, '*Qu'on se le dire*' (pass it on everybody). Henri had been the last to hold that now little-used appointment. When this much-respected man died a year later the village was faced with a crisis which was the sole topic of conversation in the bistro.

'It is quite unbelievable,' said Antoine, pushing his empty glass across the black marble table top towards the bottle of Pernod and the water jug. 'How can a sensible cultured man like our Mayor fall into such a trap?'

'He should have waited,' muttered Paul. 'A year if necessary, the right man would have come along, I am sure of it. What was the need for all the hurry?'

'It is the elections. He needs the Left Wing vote badly,' whispered Antoine, 'and remember she was once a militant Communist. Did you not know?'

'Ah,' sighed Paul, 'why should it happen to our little village? Let's face it, Henri was an honourable man, a retired police officer.'

'Yes, for twenty years he served this village. May God rest his soul.' Antoine filled his glass. 'Who is there to follow his example?'

Henri had ruled with a gentle touch. He had abundant common sense and knew exactly when it was prudent to remain at home; for instance, when Guillaume Ollier's illicit calvados still behind the brick factory blew up, all the village could smell it except Henri who was too busy 'forking fresh manure' on to his asparagus bed.

Although Henri's untimely death came as a shock to the village there was no rush of volunteers to replace him. It coincided with the arrival in the village of a cocky taxi driver from Boulogne-Billancourt, a Paris suburb. He had just completed the building of a pretentious little house on the edge of the village. The great white stone gateway with its ornate iron gates had been in place for at least three years. The villagers had got used to seeing the taxi parked outside at weekends. Now it had been replaced by a smart new Citroën which was there all week. Monsieur Leboeuf had retired from driving a taxi and was determined to become a country gentleman.

Madame Leboeuf, who had had a finger in many pies in Paris, now saw little hope that her talents would ever be acknowledged in a small village where nothing had changed for fifty years. Inevitably she picked up the news that a new *Garde champêtre* was being sought from the notice board outside the Post Office. Applicants should address themselves to *La Mairie* as soon as possible. She lost no time.

In all fairness to the Mayor, he did have misgivings that the appointment should be held by a woman. Indeed, he had never heard of such a thing. But times were changing and had he not heard that the President was decentralizing power to the regions and to mayors? Madame Leboeuf, who had had legal training like so many political activists, countered every objection he raised. She piled on the pressure by hinting that she had friends in high places within the new administration and then, with a certain amount of shameless flattery, had the job in her pocket.

The news spread like wildfire to the incredulous clients of *L'Auberge qui Chante* to cries of '*C'est affreux*' and '*Que faire?*' The next Monday morning Madame Leboeuf turned up at the Mayor's office in a splendid, tailored, blue uniform. Heavens only knows where she got it. Her hair had been cut short and a fore and aft cap sat firmly on her head. Her starched shirt was festooned with epaulettes, badges, whistles, lanyards and silver badges of rank. A broad leather belt only helped to accentuate her broad hips and sturdy legs.

74

'Where is my office?' she demanded. Madame Chauvin, cleaning the steps, looked astonished.

'Come on. Don't look so surprised,' said Madame Leboeuf. 'You know the *Garde champêtre* had an office in *La Mairie*.'

'Oh yes, Madame, but Henri stored flags there, and paint for the 14th of July.'

Madame Leboeuf snorted and strode down the corridor, trying every door in turn until she found one with the flags. She took one look.

'Filthy,' she muttered and went upstairs to the Mayor's office, where she knocked twice discreetly.

'*Entrez*,' came a voice. She marched in, clicked her heels smartly and saluted. The Mayor, who had not experienced this sort of behaviour since his military service thirty years before, did not know whether to rise, wave back or sit still and accept the compliment. He did the latter.

'I need my office cleaned out, a telephone and access to a lavatory for women only,' she demanded.

Having got his agreement, she took to the streets. This was a village where the *Garde champêtre* is seldom seen and the occasions when full uniform is worn are even fewer. This militant figure was watched with growing concern from behind lace curtains and green shutters. She planted herself in the middle of the crossroads and the village held its breath. Every solitary car was ordered to stop and then, with a shrill blast on her whistle, ordered to move on with hurried arm-waving, as if to indicate that the driver had been wasting her time. Every day for three months she stalked the village. Children who usually played outside the church in the square were ordered to go home. Young couples who used to sit on the hillside above the village washhouse were given lectures on morality and sent packing.

Madame Leboeuf believed that she had divine rights. In the best tradition of left-wing revolutionaries, she was going to rid the village of bourgeois tendencies, instil a bit of discipline and a sense of purpose into their lives. She may even have had a five-year plan, like Stalin and Chairman Mao. The village pump, that great meeting place in every French village, where the road was always partly blocked with prams, water pots and jerry cans, became her next target. A red fire hydrant was installed, but the village fire engine had connectors which did not fit. She decreed that there should be traffic circuits and then decided to change them. A week later they were altered back to what they had been. The driver of the Cooperative lorry who collected the farm produce threatened to leave the village out of his daily round if there was any more nonsense. She found a store of paint pots and began to paint white lines, dotted lines, double lines, zigzag lines. She created havoc.

The young *notaire* who lived in the village was an intelligent and articulate man who took up his law practice in the hope of leading a profitable but quiet life. He would drive home from his chambers in Versailles every day for lunch. No matter what route he took he was always intercepted by the open palm of her hand and then urged on with shrill whistle blasts. To foil her, he stopped short one day and ordered a beer and a sandwich in the *L'Auberge qui Chante*.

'It is too much. I can't stand it any longer,' he confided to every-one. 'Wherever I turn I see those dreadful ankles, squat leather shoes and outstretched hand.'

He had no need to convince his audience that a silent revolt was growing at all levels in the village.

'You must tell the Mayor that there are now ten men prepared to be *Garde champêtre*,' said Paul. 'He was in too much of a hurry when he picked her.'

'I have tried,' said the *notaire*, 'but she has a hold on him and he still hopes to be elected a deputy one day.'

'Then go and see her husband, Réné Leboeuf,' said Paul. 'He was a taxi driver and must know how to handle awkward customers.'

As the *notaire* slipped out of the restaurant to return to his office he had the satisfaction of seeing in his rear mirror an unmistakeable figure, still waiting to pounce, at the crossroads near his house. Next day he called on Réné, whose wife was distributing election leaflets, to ask his advice.

'Why do you think I began to drive a taxi?' asked Réné. 'Day and night she was engaged in politics and I just had to have a reason to be out of the house. We had been students together. It was fun. We travelled. We had much in common. But on the day she was told she would never have a child she changed to what she is today. She used to love small kids. Anyway, I shall be away for a few days to visit my mother. She is eighty-three and never did get on with my wife.'

'Who knows? This might all work out,' said the *notaire* as he left. A germ of an idea had entered his head.

76

Meanwhile, in the bistro the regulars heard news that the *Garde champêtre* would be alone.

'We must put Pierre "Le Baton" to work,' said Antoine. Pierre was the village playboy with a terrible reputation and a yellow sports car. The first night they pushed it up to the gates of her house and left. As soon as she had gone to work Pierre drove it away. The news that his car had been seen outside her house all night spread and Madame Leboeuf began to sense a different attitude among the villagers. Was it admiration or the fact that maybe she was human after all? At least it had some of the men chuckling. Two nights later the yellow car returned, pushed silently to her front door. A sharp-eyed observer might have seen an upstairs curtain move. When Pierre went to collect his car there were two parking tickets under the windscreen wipers: Contravention No. 1, Parking on a public highway without sidelights; Contravention No. 2, Parking on a double line (which had appeared mysteriously during the night).

There was a sullen silence in the *Auberge* as Pierre, Antoine, Paul and the rest realized that they were not making much headway. Outside in the street bored children who used to play in the square were being cuffed by their mothers and crying.

'The sooner I can get Max and his sister into school the better,' mused Paul. Just then out of *La Mairie* came the *notaire* and the *Garde champêtre* heading for where they were sitting. Madame rushed to the kitchen to fetch her husband to witness what had all the makings of the last scene in an American Western film. The men stiffened in their seats, the old ladies out shopping moved to a respectful distance and listened. The *notaire* was the first to speak: 'Which of you gentlemen wishes to assume the distinguished mantle of *Garde champêtre* of Crespières? Madame Leboeuf has been offered another important appointment which she wishes to undertake.'

Antoine rose unsteadily to his feet.

'If Madame wishes to transfer the honour, I will accept it.'

'Excellent, Antoine,' said the *notaire*. 'Madame Leboeuf has been invited to start a nursery school in the old forge. Just what the village needs.'

'Good, that has fixed it,' said Madame Leboeuf, moving across to where Antoine was sitting. She slammed her *képi* and whistle onto the table.

'I do not think you will need my shirt or my skirt.' She smiled sweetly, turned on her heel and strode out into the sunshine. A little later they ordered more pastis.

'It is quite unbelievable,' said Antoine. 'How can an intelligent man like myself let himself fall for that? But at least we will all be a lot happier.'

Paul rose to his feet. 'I propose a toast to Madame Leboeuf. May she now instil some discipline into our children.'

Chapter 10

CORSICAN SHEPHERDS

'Let us join the shepherds in Corsica when they move their flocks from the seashore up into the mountains,' suggested my old friend Philippe Daniel Dreyfus, who lived in France. I needed no further encouragement to escape from Herford, a garrison town in Westphalia.

We were to be guests of an ancient and much respected Corsican family, the Carlotti, who lived in a mountain village. The family was ruled by an eighty-two-year-old matriarch who still treated her sons, Paul André and Billie, both distinguished eye surgeons on the mainland in Nice, as if they were children. They ran an eye clinic in the village once a month which was free for all villagers.

Philippe described the wedding of Georges and Marise, his cousins, which lasted three days. The whole village had been invited to a stupendous banquet at which the priest, carried away by the fact that for once he had a full house, preached a tremendous sermon to the effect that the Carlotti family would not only rule Corsica one day but France too. In the middle of all this Uncle Marcel arrived from the mountain on his donkey, with three rabbits and a wild boar draped round his shoulders. At the end of the second day Marise, it seems, was still wearing her veil and crown, well down over one eye and stained with good red wine.

I had been warned that Corsica was a law unto itself and that not even the presence of the Foreign Legion was any guarantee that French laws prevailed. I drove past a grim-looking barracks. The guard on the main gate were very smart, wearing white *képis*; sergeants were distinguished by scarlet shoulder-patches. They were weather-beaten, hard, stern-looking men who were no doubt very professional, but seemed unhappy. They were not allowed to wear plain clothes off duty and there were less and less overseas stations in which they could serve.

79

I was shown round the estate, the vines and the fruit trees all beautifully maintained. At one time the population of Corsica was about 400,000, but emigration and the terrible losses of the First World War had reduced it to 200,00 in 1950. There was a great shortage of manual labour, which was overcome only by importing many men from Morocco for a few months at a time. They were good, cheerful workers, infinitely better, it seemed, than those from Algeria who were lazy and tended to squabble.

Until 1944 the lowlands at sea level had been infested with mosquitoes and malaria was inevitable. Shepherds could only graze their flocks in the cool winter when the risk lessened. After the Allies liberated Southern France in the summer of 1944 Corsica was occupied for a short time by American forces who drenched the infested swamps in DDT and in a short time it was possible to plant acres of new vines and citrus fruits. The problem, however, remained of marketing the crops, because local transport costs were higher than those of their competitors in Italy. I remember being astonished by the new irrigation systems, linked to time clocks, which all began to switch on as the sun set. We climbed into a small Renault car with a remarkable cross-country performance, through the orchards, and then a hair-raising drive into the mountains with tyres screeching round S-bends. There was hardly a bridge with its parapet intact and there were bullet holes through many traffic signs.

Next day Philippe and I joined eight other family members and we were mounted on small, sure-footed horses. We set out, after much adjustment of stirrups and girths, to climb slowly along paths shaded by cork and chestnut trees. About midday we caught up with the last of the flocks of sheep moving to fresh pastures. When we reached the grassy slopes above the forest we stopped in the ruins of a stone building for a ham baguette and a slice of cold truffle omelette. There were also about twenty semi-wild black and white pigs on this plateau who resented the arrival of the sheep and made short, snorting rushes to defend their territory. Many sows had litters, often having to hide the piglets in dense bushes until danger, such as foxes or eagles, passed. There are no wild flowers to be seen as the pigs root up every plant. The shepherd's staple diet is a heavily spiced pork *saucisson* and lamb.

These shepherd huts are usually found at the highest point where there is still fresh water. There are usually two dwellings, one for sleeping on wooden platforms and the other for cooking and living. About 300 metres away there were two piles of rocks, or 'borries', used as cheese stores. Every day the shepherds milked the sheep and began the process of making cheese. The cream was put into muslin bags to drain. The result was moulded into small circular cheeses which were stored in the stone caches. They were secured by a tiny padlocked door and I was only able to enter by crawling on my tummy. The cheeses were placed on flat rocks or planks. I counted about 1,600 cheeses which stay there for around four months. In the autumn, when the time came for the sheep to leave the mountains, the stone hides were emptied and the cheeses placed in pannier baskets on donkeys. Some of the cheese was exported to the mainland where, after special treatment, it was stored in huge caves to mature into Roquefort.

Our route took us along a narrow ridge which formed a saddle between two high peaks. The ground was thick with used cartridge cases where no doubt intrepid hunters had stood shoulder to shoulder blazing away at exhausted birds during their annual migration. The shepherds are often accused of starting forest fires in order to induce fresh grass to grow. They resent the cultivation of the lowlands and the new crops where sheep had once grazed in winter. They even resented the formation of a National Park which would repair their huts for them and even build new ones with timber flown in by helicopters.

One night we sheltered in a large mountain refuge. There were already a few travellers in the hut, including a party of noisy young Corsicans. We steered well clear of them and put our sleeping bags on a sleeping platform at the far end. As I was about to climb the ladder I was attacked by a fearsome-looking man with a knife who pulled me back and cut my cashmere sweater. My friends came to the rescue and helped me to disarm him. Eventually I climbed up to join them on the platform. I crawled into my sleeping bag and fell asleep with my heart beating fast. In my dreams I relived the scrap blow by blow. Next morning Arlette, a teacher whose sleeping bag was next to mine, said '*Roy, regardez ce que vous avez fait!*' She had the most enormous black eye and I felt sure I must have hit her in my dream. I was terribly worried and apologetic until she spared me further misery and explained that she had been bitten by a bug!

At breakfast, to the astonishment of my companions, my attacker came up and apologized, a most unusual gesture, it seems, in Corsica. He then blamed the wine and gave me a hug. We said goodbye to the shepherds and descended through some wonderful scenery until we reached a farm where we had left our horses.

There was, it seemed, one important task still to carry out. If the old matriarch was to be kept happy, then a little fish-poaching was imperative. The road followed a river which cascaded through a gorge, beneath huge overhanging rocks and into a very large pool. A small look-out party of uncles and aunts was left on the road to give early warning of the arrival of any *gendarmes*. The young mothers stood up to their waists in the water around the edge clutching satchels just below the water. The two surgeons and their children chased the fish and eels around a small island in the centre of the pool, then swam with their catches on kitchen forks to give to one of the mothers holding a satchel. When the satchels were full of slippery writhing fish we returned to the family home. Old Madame Carlotti presided over a great feast. She was obviously very proud of her clever sons, not because of their internationally renowned medical skills with a sharp scalpel, but of what they had achieved with just a blunt kitchen fork.

PART IV
1966–1980

Chapter 11

THE BERLIN WALL

Berlin, 1975

The residence allotted to British Commandants in Berlin was the Villa Lemm, built on the shores of the Havel, a great waterway which linked a chain of lakes right through the city. The Villa, however, was situated on the western edge of the divided city, barely 300 yards from the Wall which encircled as well as divided it. It was in an area of waste land and sewage farms which, when a westerly wind blew, could be smelt. It was in an area where Berliners could fly kites without infringing draconian Allied laws drafted in 1945, laws which forbade the possession of antique weapons, even replicas. During my Sunday walks I sometimes met Klaus, a semi-retired *Wachmeister* whose Aunt Hilda ran a boat-hire business in the woods by the lakeshore.

Even in a great city like Berlin there are still rural policemen. In 1920, in addition to the eight urban districts, there were fifty-nine villages and twenty-seven private estates. In 1976 there were still a few villages such as Lubars and Reinickendorf in the 185 square miles which made up the Western Sector. *Wachmeister* Klaus Wolf was responsible for about 7 square miles where there were scarcely any buildings, just woods, streams and farmland. It is an area known as the Spandau forest, not far from Spandau prison where Hitler's Deputy, Rudolf Hess, was the only occupant. If the *Wachmeister* ever regretted not having a single street on his beat he did at least have many miles of the Wall to watch and to hate.

However, it was not just the building the of wall that offended Klaus so much; it was what they had done afterwards. The German Democratic Republic (DDR: *Deutsche Demokratische Republik*) had tried to make the Wall less of an eyesore by rebuilding the section which ran through the heart of the city and which every visitor to the divided city saw and never forgot. They raised the height of the wall and painted it white. This was a heaven-sent opportunity for young West Berliners to express themselves and it was soon covered with slogans and a measure of wit which infuriated the DDR police and the occasional Russian, because they could see and hear people laughing, but they had no idea what the joke was. The Allied commandants had to prevent any further provocation in order to maintain friendly relations with the Russians.

The Communist side of the wall had also been painted. Anyone trying to escape would now be silhouetted by searchlights against the light-coloured wall, thus presenting a clear target for their machine-gunners in watch towers. As an added refinement, they placed on the top of the twelve-foot-high wall concrete drain pipes. This removed any chance of an escaper getting a fingerhold on the top of the concrete wall.

Looking down from his vantage point, *Wachmeister* Klaus Wolf could see a pair of moorhens in the reeds beneath some rusty strands of barbed wire. Whereas all vegetation on the Communist side was regularly cleared, just in case any escaper found a hiding place, the Western side of the wall was in places a jungle and invisible from the watchtowers. Five metres still belonged to the DDR and this had enabled them to build the Wall and now they could stand on it when repairs were made. Klaus had seen what democratic freedom was like in the DDR when he saw that two workmen were guarded by eight soldiers in case they made a run for it. The narrow strip was thickly overgrown and had become a haven for many different wild birds. There were Berliners living in the shadow of the Wall who made use of this strip of land to grow vegetables and placed rabbit hutches against the Wall itself. This practise had to be discouraged after the Russians launched a formal complaint on behalf of their DDR satellite.

During one particularly stormy night in November a great many trees were blown down. The next day Klaus was riding his bicycle along a track which followed the line of the Wall when he saw a most unusual bird sitting on a fallen tree. It was about the size of a black-bird and had a wide, white band around its neck. He reckoned it must be a ring ousel, swept off its migratory route by the high winds. He took another look through his glasses and saw that it was not sitting on a tree trunk; it was on a concrete pipe. Six pipes which rested on the top of the Wall had been blown off. Five had fallen into the tangle of briars and wire, but all within the 5-metre strip. One pipe, however, had rolled into West Berlin. Klaus turned round, cycled to the nearest police telephone and reported the incident. Through well-practised procedures, the information was soon being considered at the highest level. Within a few minutes decisions had been taken and the *Wachmeister* was told to wait for a British Military patrol. Twenty minutes after he had seen the ring ousel, which had since disappeared into a thicket, the patrol had arrived and he was helping them to load the pipe into the back of the Land Rover.

'Our friends over there won't like this at all,' he said to a corporal from the Royal Regiment of Wales.

'Look you, *Wachmeister*, if they ask you where it has gone, tell them they had no right to block the highway. They had better get in touch with the British Military Government,' he replied with a smile and in a strong Welsh accent.

'You should have seen the action on the other side when some West Berlin children let their gas-balloons fly over the Wall last Sunday.'

The whole incident had, of course, been observed from one of the watchtowers and was duly being reported back to the DDR authorities. However, Berlin was still under four-power control, American, British, French and Russian, who all had equal rights. The East Germans would now have to ask the Russians to approach the British. In due course we received a diplomatic note with words to the effect: 'Give us our Wall back'. The reply was delivered to the Russians in writing with a copy in German for Wolf to be relayed over the Wall by loud-hailer. The message was: 'Of course you can have your Wall back. Just come over in plain clothes with a lorry and collect it from the Military Police Lost Property Room, just like anybody else who loses something.'

The *Wachmeister* thought this was immensely funny and nearly fell off his motorbike laughing. He stopped at a spot opposite the nearest watchtower, unfastened the portable loudhailer from the pillion and relayed the message to the Vopos (East German Frontier Police). As an afterthought he added: 'and remember to sign for it in the Lost Property Book.' He wondered what the DDR reaction would be to this invitation. There was none, and seven days later the Wall was repaired, using five old pipes and one new one. The original pipe lay unclaimed for a few weeks until it ended up in the garden of the Head of Public Safety who cut it up and placed it over his rhubarb plants.

Klaus Wolf was well known to the small community he served. He had made doubly sure by giving every one of them a smart engraved visiting card with information as to how he could always be contacted. Thus it was that two small boys who had been fishing for eels knocked at his door.

'Klaus, come quickly,' called Helge, his wife, 'the boys think they have found a body, no, two bodies, in the stream beside the Wall. You had better finish your lunch and go with them.'

Klaus put on his tunic, kissed his wife and followed the boys out onto the cobbled lane. They approached the spot as discreetly as possible, not wishing to alert the Vopos, especially if either of the bodies was still alive. It only needed one excited report on the police or British Military radio to alert the East German and Russian wireless intercept service. The information would be flashed to all border posts and in no time there would be patrols with fingers on triggers and no chance of rescuing the men if they happened to be lying within the 5-metre strip.

By leaning forward over the old wire and breaking a few twigs the *Wachmeister* got a glimpse of two bodies between the stream and the wall. It looked as if they had been dead a long time. He rode back to tell his superiors, who decided that, as the bodies were so very dead, they might earn some good points with the DDR if they reported the find straightaway.

'They will have a terrible job recovering the bodies from that spot,' said Klaus to Helge when he was having his supper, 'but I bet they will try tonight.'

Sure enough, just before dusk voices could be heard on the other side of the Wall as the Vopos tramped round trying to find the exact spot opposite where the bodies lay. For most of the night that remote corner of Berlin was a scene of intense activity; there were spotlights, engines, voices, dogs barking and sounds of digging. By dawn it was all over; they had dug a tunnel beneath the Wall and dragged the bodies through to their side, put them onto stretchers and carried them away.

'Bastards,' muttered the *Wachmeister*. 'I bet they shot the poor devils and they died slowly in that miserable thicket.'

'Oh come on,' said a Military Police sergeant who had been with him most of the night. 'There has not been a shooting incident reported on this stretch of Wall for ages.'

'Well, I expect they were shot with poisoned arrows,' concluded the *Wachmeister*. In the event he was not far out, because it transpired that they were two West Berlin homosexuals who had made a suicide pact and had poisoned themselves close to their summer cottage in the woods.

Wolf pursued a hopeless and frustrated vendetta against anything to do with the Communist régime in East Germany. His sister's fiancé had been shot as he tried to escape into West Berlin and, as far as Wolf knew, was now crippled and in prison. His grandparents still lived in Rosenthal in East Berlin, where the old man had spent a lifetime working in the renowned porcelain factory. The irksome travel restrictions on visits to see them were always changing. There were queues for costly permits and the compulsory daily exchange of West German currency into Ostmarks which were worth far less and could never be reconverted. Not only did the Wall keep families apart but the import into the DDR of non-communist-approved books, newspapers, music or tapes was prohibited at checkpoints. Only western radio and television could get over the Wall, but woe betide any person caught listening to broadcasts. Klaus hated the jackboots and goosestep which had been reintroduced into their army. He despised the system by which the State controlled your life. The State dictated where each young man should work, where he could live and how much holiday he could have and where. Yet it had the nerve to call itself the German Democratic Republic. Sadly, all socialist republics, certainly in Eastern Europe and the Soviet Union, suffered from central control and restrictions.

The *Wachmeister* had fought as a youth in the last stand against the Russians on the Stossensee and Frey bridges over the Havel in 1945. He had been called up at the age of sixteen into the *Volkssturm* (Home Guard) in the last stages of the Battle for Berlin. He remembered being very frightened. After he had fired his one and only anti-tank rocket at a Russian T34 and missed he slipped away in the dusk and hid in the labyrinth of tunnels and cellars beneath the Olympic Stadium.

89

Three years later he joined the Police, where, having been brought up on a farm, he volunteered for the mounted branch. As soon as he had completed his basic training, which included six months on the beat with a fully qualified *Wachmeister*, he started work at the police stables in Spandau. This is where I first met him, when I exercised a police horse which I was going to ride on the Queen's Birthday Parade.

Wolf had never shown any desire to be promoted or to accept any unnecessary responsibilities provided he could remain with his beloved horses. After a quarter of a century, in which he won innumerable rosettes for Dressage at French Military Horse shows and trained lots of younger policemen in the art of crowd control, he was, so to speak, put out to grass. Yet he had no regrets because he loved his rural patrols in the Spandau forest, where, apart from problems associated with the Wall, he had few worries. There were, of course, Sunday picnickers who lit illegal fires, drunken parties, lost children, stray dogs chasing the deer, wild boars chasing old ladies and lusty lads chasing young ladies. But he was able to deal with all these matters in a calm, pragmatic way.

One hot summer evening, when it seemed that the entire city had taken to the woods or to the water, his little world throbbed with the din of engines, shouts and the war cries of hordes of children; Wolf had had enough. He had been on duty since breakfast without any rest and so he slipped away into the back kitchen of a little summer restaurant situated where the forest meets the upper Havel waterway. The restaurant made a little money in the winter months by providing a place where boats could be dragged ashore beneath the trees. Klaus sat down to talk to his old friend Hilda, who gave him a tall glass of lager beer and a 'bulette', which is a traditional Berlin version of a Hamburger. He had not been in the kitchen long when there were sounds of great excitement from the restaurant. Hilda went to join her husband behind the bar to find out what was happening. She dashed back into the kitchen.

'They say that there is a body lying right up against the Wall and that it is still alive,' she said, 'and the Vopos are alert but don't seem to know where it lies!'

'Oh dear,' said the *Wachmeister*, 'That is all I need to end a perfect day. If I have anything to do with it, the Vopos are not going to get their hands on that body.'

Amintire din Vizita Impĕratuluĭ Franz Josef la Sinaia.
Excursiune la Poiana Regineĭ

824 Editura George Mathéescu, Sinaia.

1. A photograph taken at Sinaia after a party given for the state visit of the Emperor Franz Josef in 1896. Princess Marie is at the top, with the Emperor on her left, King Carol on her right and her husband Ferdinard far right.

16. My mother, with her mother and two aunts at Doftana in about 1920. My mother is seated on the left.

17. "When the snow melts..."(see chapter 8).

18. Polar bears in an aggressive mood (see pp.60 & 65).

19. The author with two Corsican shepherds (see p.80).

20. The author with Philippe Dreyfus in Corsica (see p.79).

21. Bindhi, our guide and interpreter in Tibet (see chapter 13).

22. A landslide on the road from Khatmandu to Lhasa.

23. Tibetan children learning to salute (see p.109).

24. Donald Saunders and the remains of an Austin 7 in Lhasa (see p. 113).

25. The author on the banks of the River Brahmaputra near Lhasa. (see p. 110).

26. The author crossing
a bridge near
Pokara in Nepal.

27. A basket-weaver in Guyana.

28. Christmas in Guyana (see p.119).

29. General Li with his wife and two sons (see chapter 18).

30. Fish hung out to dry at Niaqormat, with a small iceberg in the middle distance. (see p.136).

31. Olga in her party frock (see p.191).

32. The Russian atomic ice–breaker *Tamyr* travelling at speed.

It was a strange phenomenon of hot summer evenings in Berlin that there was always some fool who wished to taunt the Vopos across the Wall. Some were rash enough to enter the 5-metre strip, climb onto the top and stand clutching a bottle, shouting slogans. Inevitably some lost their precarious foothold and fell on to the wrong side to be frogmarched away to many months in captivity. He wondered into what category this one might be. He left the kitchen and walked slowly towards the Wall. After a few minutes he saw that there was a crowd on the road looking at the Wall.

'Thank heavens, here is the *Wachmeister*. He will know what to do,' said a voice.

But the *Wachmeister* was far from sure. He moved to the front of the crowd and peered into the tangle of thorns and barbed wire. He could plainly see the body of a large man with his back towards them. He wore a string vest and bright blue trousers. On his upper arm Wolf could see a large blue and white tattoo. A short distance away lay a brown cap and an alpenstock.

'He will need more than that if he hopes to get anywhere,' thought the *Wachmeister*. He then looked up beyond the Wall at the nearest watchtower. The windows were all open and he could see at least four Vopos looking out with binoculars. It was unlikely they could see the body lying so close to the Wall, but they were aware something was attracting attention.

As he was contemplating what to do next, a British Military Police Land Rover arrived. The crowd appealed to the young corporal to get in there and rescue the body, which moved slightly.

'We are not allowed to step on to East German territory,' explained the young soldier in perfect German. 'If we did so and pulled that man back, whoever he is, and he may well be a fugitive from them, we would be placing in jeopardy all the privileges which exist between us and the Russians concerning our rights in Berlin.'

The corporal walked back to his vehicle and, seeing that the other side were aware of the incident, radioed a report to his operations room at headquarters. The message was intercepted by the newspapers, eager to get a story, and they sent their cameramen racing to the spot. A picture of a body being dragged over the Wall by armed border-guards was just the sort of publicity they needed to embarrass the communists. So they set up their cameras and waited.

91

'I don't think they will dare to do anything until it is dark,' said the *Wachmeister*, 'so that gives us a little more time to think up a solution.'

'Not us, mate,' said the corporal kindly, 'but if you want to risk your neck I don't expect I'll be able to see you from up by that bend. You had better get those pressmen to move. We don't want any pictures of you breaking the rules, do we?'

The *Wachmeister*'s brain was suddenly in a purposeful turmoil as he realized what the corporal had said.

'So, will you move in ten minutes?' asked the *Wachmeister*. 'I just need time to talk to my friends.' He then went to the back of the crowd where he spoke earnestly to two youths with bicycles. A careful observer might even have seen him hand them each five marks, before they pedalled off down the road, which followed the line of the Wall, and round the bend.

Three minutes later they came rushing back, shouting, 'Come quickly everybody, hurry, hurry, it's incredible, two people, the wire, the Wall, the escape ...'

Their muddled panic-stricken message was unmistakable and they got instant attention. They grabbed the Military Policemen by the arm and implored the corporal and his driver to come quickly. They started up the Land Rover and sped off towards the corner with the Press in hot pursuit.

The *Wachmeister* looked up at the watchtower. He felt a moment of acute despair when he saw nothing happening, even though he sensed some hesitation. Then all the Vopos disappeared and dropped down the ladder at great speed. As soon as they had disappeared, he plunged into the forbidden 5-metre strip. Forcing a way through the undergrowth, he tore his trousers, scratched his face and got thorns in his hands, but soon reached the body beneath the Wall. He bent down to put his hands around the man's shoulders, when the body stirred and let out an enormous belch.

'You drunken sod, you bastard, you ...' Words failed him in his anger. 'Come on, we've only got a minute to get out before they start shooting at us.'

He gave the body a kick, then dragged, coaxed, pulled and lifted the man to the road where a picnicker had opened the back of his van.

'Quick, before the others get back. I don't want anybody to know what it was I risked my neck for. Let me put my bike in too.'

The *Wachmeister* slammed the door and said to the driver as they sped away, 'The Communists will always wonder who got away and whether they are going to be punished for lack of vigilance. Heaven knows what story our newspapers will print tomorrow,' he mused. 'Let's dump that sod at the police station and then let's go back to Hilda for more beer and buletten.'

Chapter 12

THE VILLAGE FÊTE

1977, Lourmarin, Vaucluse, France
We were staying in what had once been a cave, now called La Sambuc, in the mountains of Luberon, just north of Lourmarin in the Vaucluse. Phillipe Daniel Dreyfus, a delightful Jewish Frenchman, had escaped in 1940 from the advancing Germans. He crossed into Spain and eventually joined the Free French Forces in England. His girlfriend, Colette, had fled from Paris with her friend, Juliette, on bicycles. After many days of travel they hid in a shepherd's cave. Eventually both played an important part in the French resistance movement. When the war was over Pillippe returned, married Colette and, as a wedding present, bought the cave and the surrounding land as a present for her. For the next thirty years we were lucky enough to be able to spend a little time there with them. Once a year every village in the valley had its fête.

Two canaries in a bamboo cage on a balcony overlooking the village square were singing their hearts out in delightful harmony. Their owner adjusted his large Chasseur Alpin beret to keep the sun out of his eyes and drew his chair forward so as to get a better view of events taking place below. It was a rare summer day, not a trace of the Mistral which had blown down the Rhône valley for the past three days. The climax to the annual village fête was about to start, a great three-day festival of football matches, a boules championship and children's races through the village. It was all to be directed and controlled by Gaston, the *Garde champêtre*. It was acknowledged that if anybody needed all the trappings of authority he could muster in order to control the expected crowds it was him. He wore a blue short-sleeved shirt with a tricolor shield on his sleeve. His *képi* was pushed well back on his head, so as not to disturb his sunglasses; he also carried an old, much-loved whistle on a white lanyard around his neck, which was stuffed into his belt, and khaki trousers.

There were many activities which would need his guiding hand and his vast experience of previous fêtes. And, furthermore, he was determined to provide the best entertainment. To begin with, there was always the funfair, which set up its stalls on the boulevard leading to the Château and the Protestant Church, a reminder that in this part of France there were a number of small villages whose inhabitants had been persecuted by the Popes of Avignon for their beliefs. There, beneath the trees, hung chains of coloured lights and the air was filled with an appalling cacophony of pop music, diesel generator engines and exhortations from vendors of every description. As usual, by far the most popular attractions were the dodgem cars and the *crêpèrie*, beside which there was a patient queue waiting for pancakes, bagels or just bumps. At nine o'clock in the evening the din would increase when the silver trumpet jazz band from Cavaillon would herald the start of *Le Grand Bal* in the village hall. All these activites were going to need discreet surveillance by the *Garde champêtre*.

Naturally the poor fellow could not be everywhere at the same time, so he was obliged to enlist the aid of some of his old cronies who normally worked at the Wine Cooperative. Once these red-nosed gentlemen had put on the badge of 'Deputy Sheriff', a blue and white arm brassard, they realized that for the next few hours at least they would enjoy a certain respect in the community, which was normally denied to them. They set up makeshift barricades on all roads entering the village and for the first one or two hours stood importantly beside them, refusing entry to all vehicles. They were visited and encouraged regularly by the *Garde champêtre* on his little blue motorcycle, but as the novelty gradually wore off they acquired chairs and placed them in the shade, thus continuing to exercise a show of control, albeit slightly less positive.

The fête was due to be opened with much pomp and circumstance by the Mayor. His father, Adolf, had been the only coloured general in the French Army, in charge of medical services in the Paris region. The Mayor had been born in Senegal; his father the first mayor of Dakar. Adolf would never have believed that his son might become mayor of Lourmarin. He was charming, intelligent and most amusing. It was his wife who had bicycled to La Sambuc from Paris in 1940 with our hostess Colette.

The parade was to be led by the band of the Avignon firemen, followed by the Drum Majorettes from Marseilles. These slim long-legged ladies arrived early in order to carry out a rehearsal on the *stade*, a well-worn football pitch. Unfortunately, the key to the village hall, in which these ladies were to supposed to change into their red miniskirts, blue tunics and white bearskin hats with red cockades, could not be found.

'Madame Blanc always keeps it in her handbag,' said a little girl, 'and she will not be back from Aix until the bus returns at two o'clock.'

Being accustomed to such situations, the determined damsels began to change into their costumes inside the huge green and white coach which had brought them. News travels fast in a small village. Soon all the shutters around the square began to open and balconies got dangerously crowded. Even the canaries held their breath, because it was evident to the populace that here at last was '*un veritable spectacle*'.

The ever-watchful *Garde champêtre*, seeing a crowd round the coach, rode his machine up to the window and stood up on his pedals to see what all the fuss was about. He came crashing down from his perch when an infuriated lady pushed him away with her baton through an open window. However, once he had recovered his *képi* and got his breath back, he drew his whistle and, after a few attempts, blew it shrilly, then, with good humour, proceeded to clear away the crowd and allow the girls to change in peace.

Little groups of men continued to observe from the edge of the square and kept up a running commentary for their friends not so well placed in the café. The procession began to assemble outside the town hall. The Mayor could be seen pacing up and down in his office, adjusting his tricolor sash and preparing his speech. The signal for the parade to start was the responsibility of the Deputy Marshals who were supposed to fire two *pétards*. These expensive rockets were fired from a tube whenever there was a risk that hail-stones threatened the local vineyards. They climbed to about 2,000 feet, burst above the black rain clouds and spread chemicals which would break up the clouds and save the grapes from damage. As the efficacy of these rockets was never proved, the vine growers preferred to pay for an insurance policy instead and the village had been left with a stockpile of *pétards* which the Mayor wished to sell.

The band had exhausted its limited repertoire waiting for the signal for the parade to begin. The *Garde champêtre* rode over to the car park outside the Wine Cooperative to discover that his Deputy Sheriffs were nowhere to be found. He had his own dark thoughts as to what they might be doing, but there was no time to lose. He loaded the mortars, lit a sixty-second fuse and rushed back to the parade in time to lead it off as the two bangs sounded overhead.

On the last day of the annual fête the village was entirely sealed off to traffic. A whole programme of races had been prepared for the children through the empty main street. The occasion was one of great importance to the *Garde* because it affected his relationship with the parents. The prizes had been provided thanks to the generosity of *Monsieur le Notaire* (the solicitor) and included one silver franc for each child. The course ran from the *mairie*, down past the fountain and into the *Place de la Republique*. There were races for all ages, three-legged races and egg-and-spoon races with fresh brown eggs and spoons held in tight little fists. The starter was *Monsieur le Curé*, who despatched heats of ten jostling children at a time. Whenever an egg fell off a spoon there were shrieks from the crowd and one of the many mongrels on duty that day would rush to lick up the mess.

A pile of flour sacks was brought from the *boulangerie* by the baker and handed out to children at the start point. Many of the small people disappeared inside them and subsequent races were full of spills. Everything was going with a swing when a huge white van which had found one of the barriers unmanned appeared just as a race was about to start. The cheerful, bearded driver stopped to allow the hopping children to reach the finish, which had been drawn in chalk between the café and the war memorial. Leaning forward with his feet either side of the white line was the President of the panel of Judges, none other than the *Garde champêtre*.

The van was loaded with long metal cylinders of butane gas. These were urgently needed by two restaurants and by the caterers for the Mayor's banquet. The truck would normally have driven down a little side street to deliver its belated supplies, but across the entrance to the street stretched a rope from which a bucket full of water swung gently. This was to be the site of another competition in which the losers got a bucket of water poured on their heads. The whole delicate business of erecting the apparatus had taken five men two hours to complete and many glasses of pastis in the *Café Gaby* next door. It became clear that these five worthy individuals were not going to permit the destruction of their work of art by a truck, even before it had served its purpose.

These matters, and many others, were explained to the patient driver with frequent gestures and an explanation as to how the contraption was going to work. He was reminded of the disappointment he would cause to parents and children if the event were cancelled. Anyway, why had he not delivered his load last week when he said he would? Just then he caught sight of Monsieur Guichard and his chef waiting outside the back entrance to *L'Auberge du Moulin*. The driver's tolerance vanished.

'You are a lot of old fools. What on earth does the future of a leaking bucket, let alone a childish game, matter?' he asked contemptuously. 'Either you fellows want to cook and eat or I will turn round and let you stew in your cold bouillabaisse.'

He climbed angrily back into his cab and it was clear that a momentous decision had to be made and resolved quickly, because the parents, children and spectators were getting restless at this unwanted interruption to the afternoon's sport. Once more the mantle of fate had fallen on the *Garde champêtre*. After the heated exchanges an ominous silence had fallen on *La Place de la Republique*. People gathered round or stood on their chairs to get a better view; even the canaries had stopped singing.

'It is funny how they always know when there is trouble brewing,' said an old man in a beret to his wife. The red-nosed men with the brassards on their arms closed in around their leader who pushed his *képi* further back and removed his dark glasses. He then compared the height of the bucket with that of the van. There would certainly be contact and the balcony to which the rope was tied might fall. He shook his head, then carefully looked at his watch. There was not a moment to lose.

'Bertrand, you and Jean, make a gap in the barricade there and lead the lorry across the sand where they play *boules*, then reverse into the street behind *L'Auberge du Moulin*,' he ordered his anxious deputies, 'and for heaven's sake hurry. The championship final starts in six minutes and I don't want that lot complaining.'

He turned to the driver. 'Go on, get your engine started, and when you have dumped your butane gas why don't you stay for *le menu gastronomique* and *le grand bal*?' he asked the driver, who declined the invitation and slowly followed the men clearing a way through the barricade.

A ripple of applause came from the crowd. 'Of course that is the solution!' The *Garde champêtre* blrew his whistle and at the second attempt produced two imperious triumphant piercing blasts. He cleared the crowd off the finishing line and asked *le Curé* to line up the children for the next sack race. Meanwhile, the bucket swung gently from its rope, dripping water.

'That was quite masterly,' said the old man on the balcony, as he fed the canaries from a packet of seeds. 'Our *Garde champêtre* deserves a decoration, or at least a new whistle.'

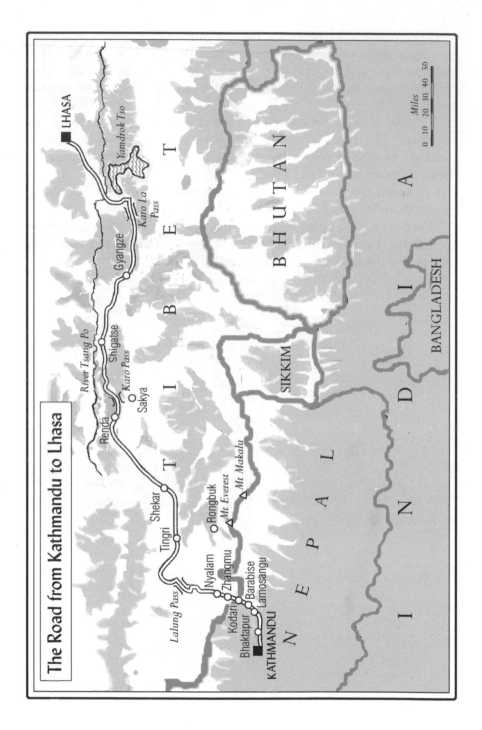

The Road from Kathmandu to Lhasa

LHASA

Yamdrok Tso

Karo La Pass

T I B E T

Gyangze

River Tsang Po

Shigatse

Karo Pass

Sakya

Renda

Shekar

Rongbuk

Mt Everest

Mt Makalu

Tingri

Lalung Pass

Nyalam

Zhangmu

Barabise

Kodari

Lamosangu

Bhaktapur

KATHMANDU

N E P A L

BHUTAN

SIKKIM

I N D I A

BANGLADESH

Miles
0 10 20 30 40 50

Chapter 13

BINDHI'S BLUFF

1982, Tibet

The trip had been months in the planning. I had even written to the Ministry of Defence seven months in advance, giving them all the details and as yet had received not a word of acknowledgement. It was nearly two years since I had retired from the army and I no longer felt that I should let them control my holidays. Now, just two days before I and my friend, Donald Saunders, and two of his friends, Tom Savery and David Callan, were due to depart I receive this letter: 'You will not be surprised to hear that they [the appropriate authority] strongly advise that you should not go to the country concerned. Although described as an "Autonomous Region", it is in effect a province of the country which was the subject of our previous correspondence. You will recall that in 1983 you recognized the need to avoid all contact with the parent country. I am advised that the visit you now propose will result in contact with them even if this will not be of your making. I very much hope you will accept the advice not to go .... If you consider there are overriding reasons why you should go you are asked to: (a) Avoid all contact with officials of the parent country; (b) Do not discuss with anyone your personal background or, particularly, your involvement with the area of your last posting; and (c) On your return give a full report of any incident which indicated an official interest in you and avoid putting yourself in a position of having to deal with different queries concerning your last visit to the parent country. It was certainly much too late to change my plans. Nothing was going to stop me now.

Donald Saunders, who I have known for over fifty years, used to live in Romania. His father was a Polish geologist who searched for oil on the fringes of the big oilfields around Ploesti with my father. Sometimes they found oil and, for a few weeks, paid off their debts.

101

Donald had made all the arrangements through Bill Cheney, who ran a travel agency in Kathmandu. I had been to Nepal on four occasions when I was lucky enough to be Commander British Forces, Hong Kong, and to have been appointed Major General, Brigade of Gurkhas. I was much looking forward to returning.

The plan was to travel overland from Kathmandu to Lhasa and back, a journey of over 2,000 kilometres, in a Chinese jeep with a driver and a Tibetan guide and interpreter. There were reports of catastrophic landslides and it was clear that we were going to have to walk some of the way. There were also reports of a shortage of food for travellers and we were going to have to do some serious shopping before we left Kathmandu. It now seemed that the biggest problem would be obtaining Chinese visas. But, for the moment, we were stuck in New Delhi airport. We were due to change flights onto a Royal Nepal Airlines flight for Kathmandu. A highly embarrassed official told us that the flight had just been cancelled because the King of Nepal wanted to go to Singapore. There were only two aircraft in the company, so we would have to wait until tomorrow. The Indian authorities were appalled because we had no visas to enter India, let alone to walk 500 metres to the airport hotel, which we could see through the window. We were put under close arrest, guarded by a police sergeant armed with a 1916 Lee Enfield bolt-action rifle. We were advised to make ourselves comfortable in the empty transit lounge.

'Spread yourselves out, gentlemen. One brown leather settee each and wait until the buffet opens in eight hours time at 6.00 am.'

This did not look promising, so went in search of a senior officer. Eventually I found one behind a brass sign saying Duty Officer. I praised the smartness of his policemen, praised the facilities in his transit lounge, 'one of the most comfortable I have ever encountered,' and noted the helpfulness of every official I had met. All this I would mention in a report I would be sending to my Queen and to his High Commissioner in London. Meanwhile, if he allowed us to sleep in an airport hotel this would enable his dedicated staff to go to bed and my dollars to be put to better use than just sitting in my pocket. He quickly saw the point and we were soon to be between clean sheets.

I began to search for tinned food, while Donald found out about Chinese visas. All I could find were pilchards, luncheon meat, whatever that might be, and beans. Not even a packet of pasta was on display on any counter. This was a most depressing start. I would have to look under the counter!

Donald told me it might take three days for the local Chinese Embassy to issue visas. It was unlikely that they could do a thorough check in Beijing on us in just three days. I hoped that they would not discover what I had been doing in Hong Kong. With a bit of luck we might be allowed to enter with the hippies and backpackers.

I welcomed the chance to have dinner at the British Embassy and catch up on the local politics and, more importantly, discover in what state was the road into Tibet. The Chinese began to build it in 1967 and it was linked to Nepal by the Friendship Bridge, just north of a hamlet called Kodari. It was a very modest structure which had not been crossed by any vehicle for many months. It was only used by porters with bulky loads on their backs. Massive landslides, I was told, had forced the Chinese to move the frontier post 1,200 feet higher up the mountain to just outside Zhangmu.

During the night I was terribly ill and eventually I was so sick in the bathroom of the Sanker Hotel that I passed out completely. Some time later Donald found me on the floor, with the top of the cistern smashed on the floor, several large pieces embedded in my thigh and my face cut.

'Not a pretty sight,' he said. 'I must get you a doctor.'

'But the bus leaves in twenty minutes,' I groaned. 'I am not going to pull out now. Help me to get clean. I'll be all right.'

I hurriedly packed my rucksack and put on my boots. In a trance I found myself on a local bus heading for Bhaktapur and the border with China. I had promised the hotel that I would be back to pay for the damage to the bathroom. It was my birthday; what a start! It turned out to be a hot, sticky day as we drove through lush semi-tropical countryside. The bus was crowded and I suddenly felt very sick. I lurched towards the front of the bus and signalled my distress, but didn't quite make it. The second time this happened a path to the door of the bus had been cleared for me. I retreated behind the bus. I felt better; there was a sense of relief among the other passengers and in no time we were bumping along from pothole to pothole. When we reached Lamosangu the road disappeared into the river, so we unloaded our kit from the bus and hired porters, who had gathered around us.

We then begin an awful walk (for me at any rate). It was very hot and we followed the river, climbing over steep little ridge after steep little ridge. Every now and again we passed little waterfalls where I stopped to fill my floppy hat with cool water and empty it over my head. After three hours we reached a village called Barbise where a red-headed Australian nurse gave me some good advice and I drank six bottles of Fanta. The road reappeared and we found a battered old taxi. This had been cut off for months from spares and maintenance and had been running a shuttle along the 20 miles of road which was still intact.

We then reached Kodari. This must be the armpit of Nepal. It stinks and is hopelessly overcrowded with travellers. There is no electricity, no standpipe or water tap and no latrines of any sort, just the left-hand side of the road as it climbs through the village. There is, however, one remarkable feature. Just below the village, beside the icy waters of the River Bhote Kosi, stood a line of porters and a few women. They were having a shower beneath a steaming waterfall, practically the only natural hot spring in Nepal. I was astonished at the physical condition of their bodies. Their shoulderblades and ribs were clearly visible, as were the red weals made by the straps of the colossal loads they had to carry daily. We clambered down to join them and stood on the rocks beneath the hot waterfall. Then we climbed in total darkness into an attic to sleep, exhausted, on bare uneven boards.

It is only a short walk to the Nepalese frontier at Kodari, where friendly officials gave us advice and a cup of tea. High up above us, at 7,000 feet we could see Zhangmu, the first town in Tibet. We passed the intrepid Colonel Blashford-Snell who was descending from his Everest base camp. He warned us not to brush against leaves because of the leeches. Zhangmu had become a transshipment centre where porters loaded up with three huge cardboard boxes at a time, filled with items such as thermos flasks, bed-covers and cooking utensils. The porters passed each other like armies of ants following an erratic and worn trail.

There is a Chinese garrison in Zhangmu and, after examining our visas, I thought that the formalities had been completed. I was wrong. Three soldiers came running after us and touched my arm. They laughed and compared my hairy arms with their smooth skins. All was well. A small bus had been provided to take us up through the village to where our jeep was supposed to be waiting. We had just climbed in when there was a low rumble and another piece of road vanished. So we unloaded our kit and began to climb again.

Eventually we were above the town and met a long line of trucks waiting for porters to transship their loads. In the distance we could see a four-wheel-drive car and at last were introduced to Mr Cheng, a tall Han Chinese, the driver and probably a security policeman as well. Beside the car there was a pink-cheeked young Tibetan girl who was to be our interpreter. She was wearing traditional Tibetan dress, had a lovely smile and was called Bindhi.

We then began an incredible drive, gradually leaving the tropical monsoon forest of oaks, maple and chestnut behind us. We climbed through an Alpine-wet forest of conifers and rhododendrons, through which the road wound ever upwards through a cleft in the mountains beside a spectacular fast-flowing river. Suddenly we were in the barren and much drier Northern Himalayas, shrubs and junipers having given way to a bleak treeless landscape of stones, spear grass jasmine and sandwort. We had reached Tibet.

It really is the roof of the world. Unlike climbing most mountains, where once you have scaled the heights you go down the other side, in Tibet you stay on top. We were not going to descend below 12,000 feet all the way to Lhasa. It is a very harsh land in which to live. There is virtually no rain. There are high winds blowing dust in your eyes. It can be bitterly cold and the wind chill factor is very serious. By day there is a relentless sun burning out of a cloudless sky. It is a land with little to eat, especially for travellers. It is a land of lichens, moss, a little barley, sheep, yaks and horses and, for people like ourselves, there is always exhaustion due to High Altitude Sickness. This can begin at about 10,000 feet.

We reached Nyalam, 12,000 feet, at dusk and immediately felt the effect of altitude sickness as soon as we carried our kit into a hotel which was still under construction. We were shown into a room with wood shavings on the floor, but there were beds and mattresses. What a joy, but there was also a feeling of general weakness and shortness of breath, headache, nausea, dry cough, catarrh and loss of appetite, all symptoms our guide book had warned about. Outside in the road there was a tremendous row. A man was being denounced by his wife in front of a small crowd of laughing citizens. He was then dragged away by two men and I wondered what it was all about.

Tibetan history is not recorded before the seventh century and the next 1,000 years are a complicated tale of invasion by Chinese, Mongols and Gurkhas. British links began in 1780, although only the Indians were allowed to trade. After an incident on the border with Sikkim, the tutors of the 7th Dalai Lama went to see Tsar Nicholas of Russia to ask for his help. This thoroughly alarmed the British in India, who always feared that Russian influence might spread south into India. They sent Colonel Younghusband with a small force into Tibet and he succeeded in establishing permanent trade and telegraphic links with India. Before pulling out in 1908, the British agreed with the Russians that it should be the Chinese who really exercised sovereignty over Tibet.

In 1912 the 13th Dalai Lama proclaimed Tibet an independent nation. Sadly, no other nation recognized the fact. The British preferred to call Tibet an autonomous country within the Chinese sphere of influence. So Tibet ran her own affairs and stayed neutral in both World Wars. The British withdrawal from India in 1947 encouraged China to 'liberate' Tibet and thousands of settlers and troops moved in. In 1958 the Tibetans revolted. Their hopeless struggle ended with the flight of the 14th Dalai Lama over the mountains into India. China declared Tibet an autonomous region of the People's Republic of China. A year later the terrible excesses of the 'Cultural Revolution' spread to Tibet and the ruins of that orgy of destruction are still visible.

We set off early next day and crossed a treeless plateau covered with moss and a few tufts of grass, amongst which some sheep grazed. The ruins of the monasteries destroyed during the Cultural Revolution still stood out, like trees struck by lightning, in this lunar landscape. At one time there were 4,600 monasteries; now there are just ten, which have been partially restored. The Chinese Ambassador to London wrote a well-reasoned letter to *The Times* in 1987 in which he said that 200 were going to be rebuilt.

As for the lamas (monks), it seems that they were reduced from about 11,000 to 1,000. I have been reminded that few religious groups in the world have ever equalled the power and influence exerted by the lamas over the poor people of Tibet.

It took us thirteen hours to drive from Nyalam to Shigatse along a dusty track without any sign of life or another vehicle. We climbed up

106

to the Lalung Pass at 15,500 feet, from where we could glimpse Mount Everest and other peaks covered in snow. The car could not make it and shuddered to a halt. Total silence followed, from both the engine and us, the passengers. The thought of being stuck on this mountain with a tin of pilchards was too awful to contemplate. There was trouble with the petrol pump, no oil in the air filter; the engine had been starved of air and fuel. Mr Cheng selected various tools to get at the trouble. A final blow with a yellow-handled hammer and we were once more in business. We descended into a rolling, rocky countryside where herds of yak, sheep and cattle grazed. The peasants waved and, whenever we stopped, came running up asking whether we had any postcards of the Dalai Lama. The importation of such seditious material was discouraged by the Chinese. The children, however, were more pragmatic; they wanted biro pens and then sweets, in that order.

The people of Tibet are being swamped by the Chinese and by their culture. In time they may become an endangered species. It used to be said that they could be divided into five general categories: (1) noblemen: very few, if any, remain in the country; (2) merchants: in towns, losing ground to the Chinese settlers; (3) farmers: the most numerous, who seldom own the land they farm; (4) nomads and herdsmen: living on high-altitude steppes; and (5) outcasts: who dispose of bodies, human and animal.

The children are good-humoured and seem to be adapting much more easily to the social changes forced upon their parents.

We slept in a barracks which we reached after dark and where there was no electricity. Outside the building in which we slept there were at least ten wild dogs, loose and barking. Somewhere in the pitch darkness beyond the dogs there was, so Bindhi told me, a latrine pit but there was no thunder box to sit on or bar on which to perch. I was terrified of falling in.

After a hideous night we set off. We must have reached a Chinese sphere of influence because Bindhi no longer wore her Tibetan national dress but was in jeans and a T-shirt. Mr Cheng wore a dark suit without a tie.

The road was still unsurfaced and would remain so until we got near Lhasa. Every few miles there were teams of women holding long-handled shovels and pushing wooden wheelbarrows, trying to fill in the potholes. We drove for another hour before we saw another vehicle which was followed by a huge dust cloud that settled on us.

At milestone 483 there was a military checkpoint where, curiously, the soldiers took little interest in us foreigners. They asked Cheng and Bindhi lots of questions about their movements.

'If you try to avoid the checkpoints,' whispered Bindhi, 'they will chase you with rabid dogs.'

Bindhi was twenty-one, she had learnt English at the Chinese University in Beijing, so it was not surprising that her knowledge of English was, at best, superficial and her comprehension of the spoken word minimal. Whatever I said or asked she replied 'Yes' with a sweet smile, but both she and I knew that she had not understood a word. We were her first clients and she had to be one of the very few Tibetans to have been entrusted with a job and a chance to earn some money. We all took good care not to let Mr Cheng, who was probably some sort of Chinese official, know just how weak her English was.

We managed to persuade them to agree to a deviation of 50 kilometres south to the ancient monastery of Sakya. It is one of the best-preserved, and, possibly because it lies off the beaten track, escaped the orgy of destruction in 1959 when 1.2 million Tibetans were killed or died of cold and starvation. It was built in the eleventh century and became the centre of the 'red-hat sect' of lamas, with close links to the Mongols and Genghis Khan. This is reflected in its architecture. Inside, there is a marvellous collection of artefacts, but it is all in semi-darkness and under a thick layer of dust. There is a wooden horse covered in leather and copper armour which must have weighed at least 100 pounds. I ran my hand along the top of a wall and found a suit of chain mail, two curved swords and a strange helmet with a red plume.

Our visit was a sad one for Bindhi because it was the first time she had been able to return to the village where her grandfather was killed, putting up a futile resistance to the Chinese. When we collected her from beside the new bridge over the river below the village she could hardly keep back her tears. She was prevented from telling us what had happened by the presence of Mr Cheng.

We drove for a few miles and then stopped for a picnic beside a river. We were soon joined by some children who watched every mouthful we took in silence and from a respectful distance. We found the scrutiny hard to bear and gave Bindhi a packet of biscuits to distribute to the kids, who by now had been lined up and taught how to salute like guardsmen. I took a photograph. Their clothes were dirty and torn. There was a great shortage of buttons, but their smiles were truly rewarding.

We drove on to Shigatse, a town of 40,000 people, which contains the Trashilhunpo Monastery. This was built by the first Dalai Lama in 1447. Shigatse was once the official residence of the Panchen Lama, who is now held as a sort of hostage by the Chinese in Beijing. He is second in importance to the Dalai Lama, who, after his escape, went to live mostly in India, sometimes in New York.

We followed pilgrims who walked clockwise round the monastery, prostrating themselves every few steps as they circumvented the steep hill on which it stands. A cheerful family group invited us to share their food; it was a very kind gesture from people who have practically nothing to offer.

We now entered a fertile valley and drove to Gyangze, a small town dominated by a fourteenth century fort. This was captured in 1905 by Colonel Younghusband with a force of Gurkhas and Royal Fusiliers. They fought the world's highest battle when they managed to outflank 3,000 Tibetans who were entrenched on the Karo Pass at 17,000 feet. The British occupation did not last long. They left behind a Field Post Office and a wool agent, whose task may have been to provide wool for the Royal Navy. They may even have provided yak hair for the helmets worn by the Household Cavalry in London.

We halted at the top of the pass, where a glacier stops short of the road. There is a profusion of rock jasmine, gentians and a few patches of green grass on which two wild yak were grazing. These are enormous animals, weighing over a ton, brown in colour, relatively rare and are called 'dong' by Tibetans. The domestic yak is smaller and has a black shaggy coat. The females are called 'dri'. Yak are used to draw ploughs or to carry 160 pounds in saddlebags. They give a very rich milk, which makes butter or can even be used as fuel oil for lamps.

Every monastery seems to have a large quota of dogs. There are dozens of shaggy, contented dogs asleep in courtyards and on steps. They are supposed to be the reincarnation of monks who did not quite make it to heaven last time round and are now on their best behaviour. There must have been at least thirty dogs inside the Palkor Monastery at Gyangze in which there is a unique eight-sided, nine-storey-high *chorten*, or pagoda, on which there are 1,000 images of Buddha. I told Bindhi that I found the dogs easier to understand.

The dusty road to Lhasa descends to the Yamdrok Lake, which, at 14,000 feet, must be among the highest in the world. We looked down on a huge clover-shaped expanse of black water. In this fresh-water lake are fish without any scales. There is no sign of life, not a boat, not a house, not even a bird.

After following the shore for 20 kilometres, there was a boatman about to ferry provisions to a distant village from which a thin plume of smoke rose. He lifted a huge bundle of wool and a sack of grain into a coracle, which had been constructed by stretching yak skins over a frame of willow and thorn. Bindhi explained that he belonged to a caste of so-called outcasts because he had to butcher and skin the yak. We watched him climb in and start paddling towards the distant shore, sitting awkwardly on the edge of the boat.

Further on, the road was blocked by a convoy of Chinese military trucks which had halted beside a 'jeep' which was upside down in a ditch. We waited about an hour and a half until some Chinese military police arrived. They then took measurements and picked up a piece of bumper, a headlamp and some broken glass which in no way blocked the road to traffic. I joined some spectators at a discreet distance from where we watched the charade of a painstaking investigation being played out.

A Tibetan herdsman borrowed my binoculars and pointed out with pride his six horses grazing in a meadow beyond the roadblock. Eventually we moved on and started to climb the last pass before the valley on which Lhasa stands.

Lhasa is dominated by the Potala Palace, one of the most impressive buildings in Asia. It is like a giant Windsor Castle on top of a red rock. It is a sacred place and its name means High Heavenly Realm. There were 900 rooms when it was built in the seventh century. Then it gradually fell into decay until it was almost a ruin when, in 1645, the 5th Dalai Lama decided to rebuild the palace and the Potala became the traditional residence of all subsequent Dalai Lamas. It also became the seat of national government, the treasury, library, ammunition depot, state prison and torture chamber. The Chinese shelled it in 1959, but inflicted less damage than a drastic fire caused by an electrical fault in 1984 or the resident army of wood-boring insects. It is an amazing construction of stones, earth, clay, lime and timber, in which there is not a single nail. Apparently, it is also resistant to earthquakes because, when it was built, there was an empty central core into which molten copper was poured.

We had been dropped off at No. 2 guesthouse and said goodbye to Bindhi and Mr Cheng. She had removed all traces of Tibetan dress and wore a new T-shirt and jeans.

We set off to explore the city, whose population had now risen to over 150,000. There were many ugly, new functional buildings used by Chinese settlers and a large military garrison. A few modern hotels had been built, which even supplied oxygen masks above the beds for use by those intrepid travellers who had flown in from California for a weekend. This is far too short a time to get acclimatized to the high altitude, so many suffer unexpected discomfort. The old religious and geographic centre of Lhasa is the Jokhang Temple, built in 650. This contains the statue, or image, of Sakyamuni, one of the many names of Buddha. The Red Guards did not attempt to destroy this temple and for a while it was used as No. 5 guesthouse.

Around the temple there is a thriving street market, which must be walked round clockwise, taking great care to avoid the many pilgrims who prostrate themselves on the ground every 2 metres. Some have been walking for months in order to visit the Potala once in their lifetime. They are almost destitute and sell their precious personal ornaments to buy enough food for the long journey home.

I am intrigued by an old lady who takes only five steps before falling to the ground. She places her foot on a rope, which secures a sheep to her ankle, before kneeling down and, with great difficulty, pushes herself forward, raises her arms, which sweep the ground down to her waist, then presses up to another kneeling position. The sheep settles down beside her, between each prostration, patiently waiting for the next move. When the old lady reaches the temple she removes her headgear and various ropes bound round her body before praying. I could only feel humble in the face of such faith and determination. It was outside the Jokhang Temple that anti-Chinese demonstrations began in 1987.

There are rows of monks from distant provinces, who sit on the pavement waiting for their bowls to be filled with a lumpy rice porridge dished out from a container on a pushcart by a temple official wearing western-style clothing. They add twigs to a massive brick incense-burner and spoonfuls of a scented white powder. There are cheerful, attractive Tibetan girls in traditional clothes, who intercept foreigners leaving the market. They are selling jewellery in exchange for foreign currency vouchers. This capitalist venture is nipped in the bud by the Chinese security policemen with hatchet faces who wear black leather jackets. At every stall the seller quotes a price, then writes it down on his wrist with a biro pencil or uses a pocket calculator. You halve the figure, and so it goes on. You give them foreign currency and they try to give you change in local currency. These people are as sharp as any in the world.

The meat stalls are gruesome; the butchers stand beside huge hunks of yak meat. Beneath the tables there are sheep and yak heads and bundles of tangled yak hair. Some of the meat has been spiked onto the iron railings which surround the market. There are dogs everywhere, but none dare touch the meat unless it has been given to them. There are piles of skins lying in the dust. Nothing, it seems, is ever wrapped up.

Apart from the Chinese and Tibetan communities, there are a tiny group of Muslims who have their own green and white mosque. They seem to be employed in restaurants and shops. I notice that none of the vegetable stalls sell any fruit other than small, firm, red apples. Among the vegetables are enormous turnips, beans, spinach and squat-looking cabbages. Donald Saunders remarks that there are no tin-openers, pens or pencils and that everybody walks clockwise round the bazaar.

We have both bought a replica Chinese military uniform for our children. A ragged boy approaches begging in English, 'I want money, I have no parents.' Tibetans laugh at this up-market approach; the lad smiles; I wait until he has learnt to say 'thank you' and then I give him something.

On our last day Bindhi unexpectedly turns up without Mr Cheng. She is very worried because the Chinese who run the tourist bureau are going to check with us how well can she speak English and whether we are satisfied with her as a guide. She explains that if she loses her job she will never have another chance. Can we please help her? Of course we can and we sing her praises to two stern officials in dark suits who tick our replies on a buff-coloured form.

Tucked away on the edge of the city is the Norbulongka, or the Jewel Park, an oasis of flowers and shady trees created in 1755 by the 7th Dalai Lama, who built the first Summer Palace. A new modest palace was built in 1950 and it was from here that the 14th Dalai Lama fled from Chinese attack nine years later, leaving everything behind, including three cars. According to an old guidebook, these had been given to his predecessor by the British in the 1930s, a Buick and two tiny Austin Sevens, which were carried through the mountains in pieces from India. When I asked if the cars were still there no Chinese official had an idea what I was talking about. So we hunted around and eventually found them in a timber yard behind the summer palace, two bright yellow Austin Sevens and the large American car with a small tree growing out of the centre of the chassis. Bindhi sat behind the wheel in the rusty Buick, wearing a blue straw hat which she had just bought. She looked splendid.

As Mr Cheng was not with us, we asked her about life in Tibet. It was quite difficult to decide from what she said whether they were better off under the Chinese than under the lamas. Drepung Monastery, outside Lhasa, controlled 700 other monasteries and literally thousands of monks. They all had to be maintained and fed through taxes. The good land belonged to the lamas, who paid no taxes and who did no work outside the monastery. So it fell to the luckless village headman to collect the taxes needed to support the monks.

The people had no say whatsoever in the government of their district, but now the Chinese claim about 50 per cent have a say in the government. However, it is clear that they are closely supervised by their Han Chinese superiors and, in spite of the new roads, hospitals, electricity and social changes, the Tibetans yearn to be able to govern themselves in the bad old ways.

As we set off on our return trip we discover that Bindhi's father is a doctor in Shigatse and that tomorrow is his birthday. The one thing he desires most is a pair of shoes. Donald and I give her some money and she slips off to the hospital where he works while we look at the market. The look on her face when she returns tells us all.

Five days later we said farewell to Mr Cheng and to Bindhi at Zhangmu. We gave them all we could spare. She had earned her spurs, so to speak, on her first assignment and it was a sad farewell. We hurried past the Chinese frontier post and past a group of boisterous soldiers. It was easy to understand the Tibetan point of view. We walked down the mountain path to meet the friendly Nepalese and their teapot. Later in the day I found a piece of paper, slipped under the flap of my pack, on which was written in bold cautious letters 'Mr Roy, Tank you, I will forget not. Bindhi.'

And, of course, nor will I.

Chapter 14

THE AMERINDIANS

1973, Guyana, South America

Our project at the National Defence College of Canada was the colonial legacy left by Portugal, Spain and England in South America. We visited Brazil, where I remember the extraordinary new capital city, Brasilia, recently built, in which few people at that time wished to live. I shall never forget the golden beaches of Rio de Janeiro or the hundreds of sun-tanned young people. By sharp contrast, Bogotá, capital of Colombia, seemed to be a dangerous and unhappy place, but it contained the unique gold museum where gold is piled high from floor to ceiling.

It had taken the Royal Canadian Air Force an hour at 300 knots to cross the Amazon Delta. The Demerara River, which flows through Georgetown, the capital of Guyana, is just about as brown as the sugar from which it takes its name. Over 1,000 years ago the country was inhabited by Arawak and Carib tribes. The present name, Guyana, is a native Amerindian word meaning 'Land of Many Waters' and lies between the Amazon and Orinoco Rivers. The Amerindian is the aboriginal inhabitant of Guyana and is sometimes known as a Buckman. In folklore they were considered to be very primitive and the term Buckman conveyed the idea of stupidity. A widely-used metaphor is 'Buckman Distance'. If an Amerindian says that some place is 'jus dung deh', meaning not far away, he might mean it is 2 or 10 miles away, or even that you may have to walk all day and not get there until dark. The Amerindian male is bone idle except when hunting or fishing, building or defending his home. It is the women who plant the bitter cassava, their staple diet. Women reap the crops, prepare the food and look after the children. When an Amerindian shoots an animal he leaves it where it fell, then goes home where he climbs into his hammock, lights his pipe and has a smoke. His wife and children are directed to where the carcass is lying and they are expected to gut it and carry it back.

The Amerindian is a fisherman who does not use a rod and line or a net as we do. He usually stalks his fish and shoots it with a bow and arrow, but he might block a stream at a narrow point and then throw curare, a poison made from the bark of a tree, which soon brings panting fish to the surface where he collects all he needs. I developed an admiration for these resourceful men.

It had been a long uncomfortable flight from Brazil in a Canadian military aircraft and I was only too happy to be able to wander around the city. Furthermore, we all had a purpose, which was to buy a shirt. We had on arrival been presented with a formal invitation to dine with the Prime Minister, Mr Forbes Burnham. We were advised that the code of dress was to be 'Jump up' shirt. 'What on earth is that?' we had asked. The garment turned out to resemble a bush jacket. I soon realized that this was only to be obtained from one shop, possibly enjoying the great man's patronage. I was reminded of King Carol II of Romania who in 1938 insisted that all officers should have a handkerchief bearing his portrait and the only factory which made them was owned by the King. I still have my bright yellow shirt which I have kept for over thirty years.

The coastline of Guyana was first visited and mapped by Spanish sailors in 1499, who were searching for the fabulous lost city of El Dorado. They were followed by Dutch and Portuguese explorers who established various settlements, but lost them to the more aggressive Spanish. The Spanish did not get on with the indigenous Amerindians and fought a number of battles against them. The Spanish continued to pursue them for many years. The Dutch, on the other hand, made friends with the Amerindians and firmly established themselves. In 1621 the Dutch West India Company was granted a charter to plant sugar cane and coffee, profitable crops which were sold in Europe.

In 1650 the first slaves were brought from West Africa to work on the plantations. By 1742 other Europeans were attracted by the abundant harvests and the opportunity to get rich using a cheap labour force. For forty years the governor of Guyana was Laurens Storm van Gravesande. African slaves were treated with increasing barbarity by the European planters who were vicious and exceedingly cruel, knowing that their inhuman conduct would never be made known in their home countries. The slaves, however, did revolt, and one case is still remembered as the Berbice Rebellion. The slaves took control of one plantation for nearly a year before being suppressed.

Slavery was abolished by decree in 1834. The Africans, while still continuing to serve an apprenticeship on the plantations, began to assert their independence and established their own villages away from the estates. This left the planters with a much reduced labour force. They were then obliged to develop a system of contract labour which recruited immigrants mainly from India, but also some from Madeira, China and Malta. This still tied labourers to the whims of planters, but only for a set period. In 1917 this too was abolished and ten years later the power of planters over labourers was reduced still further, in line with the Crown Colony System of the British Government. The country at last began to make rapid constitutional progress and in 1953 went to the polls for the first time. The result was a huge victory for the People's Progressive Party led by Dr Cheddi Jagan whose family and supporters were of Indian descent. It was also the height of the Cold War and Dr Jagan's earnest desire to form a Marxist state resulted in the constitution being suspended. An interim government was formed.

After ten turbulent years another election was held under a system of Proportional Representation and a Coalition government was formed. Mr Forbes Burnham, leader of the People's National Congress, whose supporters were mainly African, became Prime Minister. The nation became independent on 23 February 1970, the only Co-operative Republic in the Commonwealth. To complete the picture, they elected as President Mr Arthur Chung, who was of Chinese descent.

At the dinner, which was most entertaining, I sat next to the leader of the opposition, Dr Cheddi Jagan. There was light-hearted rivalry between the two main political parties which resulted in a bread roll pitching onto our table from the direction of the Prime Minister's table. The ensuing bombardment only ended when both sides had run out of ammunition. The menu included curried hassars, which, I believe, were some kind of prawn; they turned out to be quite delicious.

St George's Anglican Cathedral, right in the centre of the city, is believed to be the largest wooden building in the world. Painted white, it stands in the middle of a roundabout and people dodge the traffic to enter it. I got there just as a wedding finished, and was befriended by Samuel, who was anxious to tell me about Guyanan marriage customs. It seems there is an eve of wedding celebration in the home of one couple. It is called the Queh-Queh dance, can go on from three to five hours and is performed mainly by women. They form a ring with the bridegroom or bride in the middle. The dance is interpretive and most suggestive, depicting the copulation expected of them later. Everybody takes it in turn to dance in the circle with the intended spouse. There is lots of gyratory footwork and waist movement and lots of Queh-Queh songs. He gave me a song sheet which meant little to me:

> 'Anyway Sancho call you ('Nack am dung' after each line)
> If a dam an all
> If a trench an all
> If a roadside self-self
> If a house top self-self.'

Samuel sang a few lines and clapped his hands. He also told me that when an Amerindian child is born the mother puts the baby into a river. If the baby floats she takes it out of the water and rears it. If it sinks she leaves it because it means that the child will never be able to save its life by swimming when it gets older; so why bother now? It was a logic I could not follow.

Just before I said goodbye to Samuel, he pointed to two men with weather-beaten faces and huge hands. 'Those men are pork-knockers.' This, he explained, was the accepted way of describing miners who were gold-diggers or diamond-seekers. The name originates from the fact that their staple diet, when travelling in the interior, was pickled pork and pickled pig tail. Even when fresh meat was available it was invariably wild hog that they ate.

In Creole the word 'knock' sometimes means to eat; for instance they might say, 'Me knack salt poke an rice fur breakfus today.' Because pork was the main ingredient for cooking and by far the most expensive foodstuff, it was only when he had struck it rich that a miner could knock on a shop-counter and demand his 'salt poke'. Hence the terms 'knock' or 'pork-knocker' originated. Of course, those less fortunate tried to flavour the pot by tying string around a pork bone and dunking it in the stew. Poor peasants in Russia who could not afford sugar used to tie a thread round a sugar lump, dip it in every cup of tea, then hang it in a corner cupboard. It was said that when there was no sugar left they would just look at the cupboard before drinking their tea.

It was a very hot day and an open-topped sedan drove by, with music from Radio Demerara blaring out. Sitting on the top of the back seat was Father Christmas. I walked past Guyana's leading funeral parlour and mortuary, 'specialists in embalming and shipment overseas'. Catering for tourists, no doubt, with Canadian-designed caskets. Canada has considerable interests in the bauxite mines managed by Alcan. There were also the Green Shrimp discotheque, the Zanzibar night club and the Seventh Day Adventists, who seemed to have taken over, with seventy-four churches and thirteen schools.

As we began the twenty-five mile drive to the airport at Timehri we stopped to take on board five crates of Demerara Rum, a personal gift from the Prime Minister. How we were going to get them past the Customs in teetotal Ontario was another problem. But gifts should be accepted graciously. On a previous handover of barracks between regiments in Georgetown, the outgoing commanding officer of a British infantry regiment from East Anglia took great pains to make sure his barracks was spotless. He explained that the men must make their own entertainment and handed over a makeshift theatre and stage, which they had constructed in a disused warehouse, to the incoming battalion of Foot Guards. The accommodation and equipment had all been accounted for, less the traditional pokers, fire, one deficient, and deemed to be in good condition. Just as he was about to drive off he turned to the immaculate Lieutenant Colonel in the Guards, 'Oh, by the way, you will find it pretty lonely being in command out here. I have a small present for you which should make your time in this place a lot more amusing. You will find it in that little bungalow at the bottom of your garden. She is called Pineapple!'

Chapter 15

THE DOWAGER DUCHESS

1980, La Sambuc

'I have it on command from Her Majesty The Queen to convey to you on leaving the Active List of the Army her thanks for your long and valuable services. May I take this opportunity of wishing you all good fortune in life. Signed Francis Pym, Secretary of State for Defence.' So that is that. I am free to do as I wish, or so I imagine. All I now need is a job and a home, but before I start looking, I take a few days' leave with my wife, Valerie, to visit our favourite corner of Provence, the Luberon. It dawns on me that, from now on, I do not have to call it 'Leave'.

For many years I had brought a tin of Three Nuns tobacco for Monsieur Blanc, whose ramshackle farm lay in the valley below La Sambuc. He lived there with his daughter, Violette, who ran the post office in Lourmarin with his old mother. He wore a splendid, wide, straw hat, with a piece missing from the brim, which looked as if one of his goats had taken a bite. He knew that I coveted his hat and promised to find one for me.

His mother, Gabrielle, had been ill, with a painful growth pressing down on her forehead. The doctor from Aix-en-Provence was called. He practised leechcraft and brought with him a small cardboard box containing *une sangsue* (a leech). The box was opened by the doctor and the hungry beast was strapped above the swelling on her forehead. This well-tried remedy relieved the pressure. Canny business-man that he was, Monsieur Blanc told me that, if you are smart, the blood in the leech can be squeezed out and the leech used again, thus only paying for one treatment.

Monsieur Blanc, who wore a belt and braces, could barely scratch a living from four small fields and a vineyard on the slopes of the valley. He did, however, have a neglected water reservoir which was surrounded by brambles and was now in a bad state of repair. One year, when the swimming pool at La Sambuc failed, we were able to swim in its fresh, cool water from the mountain. Next year it will probably be dry and, as he has stopped growing melons, it probably will not be needed.

Once a week the bank Credit Agricole opened its door in the *Rue d'Apt*, beneath the chestnut trees. It was the only bank in the village and dispensed money and advice in equal measure for three hours a week. It was a little bit like a consultant's waiting room. There were chairs, magazines and copies of *Le Provencal*, the local edition full of bicycle races and football match results. The first customer was a young mother who walked her young daughter every morning 3 kilometres down to the village school and back again in the afternoon. The cashier was a friendly blonde, wearing a bright yellow T-shirt. She was very welcoming but insisted that I sit down and wait until she was ready. She was trying to communicate with her computer which failed to show the exchange rates for the day. Success at last, I cashed my traveller's cheques, a swift transaction, and said goodbye to everybody who was still waiting, as seemed to be the custom.

A few days later, having breakfast in the shade of the green oak at La Sambuc, my hostess, Colette Dreyfus, announced, 'Today we are having lunch chez la Duchesse. We must all remember to call the Duke *Seigneur*'. We hardly got going at all; as usual, the keys to the little green Renault were missing. We went down in third gear through a forest of green oaks and pine, bouncing over a mesh of tangled tree roots which spread like a monster's ribs across the track. We then drove at breakneck speed past vineyards, orchards and olives. In the heat of the day there was nobody to be seen. In the distance we glimpsed the twelfth-century Château of Ansouis built on top of an even older fortress between the Luberon Mountains and the River Durance. We left the steaming car outside the wine co-operative. The water level, it seemed, had not been checked since last summer. The manager of the Ansouis Co-operative had blending skills which made his wines the best for miles around. He had a cup attached to a long rod which he dipped into each enormous vat to provide a sample. We chose the red and the rosé and then waited while he completed a certificate which allowed us to transport 40 litres in a private motor vehicle.

We walked to the base of the rock and started the climb to the château, up wide stone steps and a ramp into an impressive chestnut avenue leading to the castle entrance. The massive door was decorated with pyramidal bosses which Philippe tried to polish with his jacket sleeve. Above the door there was a beautifully carved Sabran family coat of arms. We were ushered inside and climbed a vaulted grand staircase to an anteroom on the first floor. The walls were covered with portraits of the Sabran family through the ages. Every small table was covered with a selection of ornaments and silver gifts presented by some Emperor, but by which?

The butler announced the entry of the Duke. Colette, staunch Republican that she is and holder of the *Croix d'Honneur*, was about to curtsey to the floor but changed her mind when she noticed his trousers. The Duke is a young man wearing brightly coloured Harlequin-striped trousers and a black silk shirt. A lion's claw hung from a gold chain around his neck. The Dowager Duchess now made her entrance through double doors at the far end of the room. She was very gracious, quite like the British Queen Mother. It was soon apparent that she was a great character and that she spoke excellent English. She gave a little nod and drinks were offered.

Suddenly, her daughter the Duchess of Orleans, joined us, breathless, having run up the grand staircase two steps at a time. She was a charming, vivacious blonde who captured my attention, but she had a companion in attendance. It turned out that he was the pretender and heir to the throne of Portugal, a pleasant young man with a drooping moustache, a grey shirt and two ball pens clipped to his pocket. The party was finally completed by a Dutch schoolmistress from Bergen-op-Zoom, dark, dumb and completely overawed.

We cross into the dining room in which hang two seventeenth-century Flemish tapestries depicting the story of Dido and Aeneas about which I dared not reveal my ignorance. We eat off gold-crested plates and with crested cutlery. The hors d'oeuvre is a delicious selection of mushrooms, quail's eggs, small sausages and baby carrots. This is followed by a silver serving dish covered in packets of tinfoil. 'Beware', says the Duke. 'One of them is empty. The rest contain aubergines stuffed with chopped veal and cheese.'

During lunch we listened to an incomprehensible story about Field Marshal Montgomery who apparently came to lunch when he was the Deputy Supreme Commander, Allied Forces, Europe. It concerned the possible theft of a silver spoon. The chief suspect, it seems, might have been his ADC, whose family were in some way related to the Duchess and whose crest resembled that of the Sabran family.

After lunch we were shown the Dowager Duchess's bedroom and her roof garden, with fabulous views over the village and the mountains beyond. There were four doors out of the bedroom but none led to a bathroom. A little Yorkshire terrier, obviously a very privileged animal, sat on the bed. Finally we were shown a little boudoir which smelt strongly of lavender and drains. The old lady told me that she would love to read *The Rise and Fall of the English Nanny*. I offered to try to find a copy, but, to my shame, I failed until twenty-five years later when my wife, Valerie, discovered one at the back of a bookcase.

We drove back to Lourmarin at a much more leisurely pace, via the castle ruins in Cadenet where we had once tried to catch swallow-tailed butterflies using the knickers of the three small daughters of Richard and Mrs Vickers. We stopped for a cold beer on the shady side of the street in the centre of the village. Monsieur Bernard lurched down the street towards us; he steered an erratic but rapid course for the *Café Gaby* which he visited about four times in the course of a working day. He had an enormous walrus moustache, an untrimmed beard and translucent pink cheeks. His nose was almost purple, probably caused by prolonged immersion in a glass of *Ricard pastis*. There was a time when he owned the grocery which his long-suffering daughter now ran almost single-handed. He still helped her to unload heavy trays of melons, sacks of potatoes and trays of chickens. A visit by the local hygiene inspector last year had caught him on a bad day. He resented the suggestion that, just because a few cockroaches had gathered beneath the refrigerator and none of the work-surfaces had been cleaned since Pentecost, the store might have to be closed. The inspector rashly demanded to be shown the cold meat store. Monsieur Bernard obliged, gave him a shove and closed the door. He then went off to enjoy a second glass of *pastis* and get over what must have been a stressful morning. The pitiful cries of the unfortunate inspector and his bangs on the door were eventually heard by Réné, the hairdresser, who released him. The rest is history!

Chapter 16

GUARDS OF HONOUR

I've got a lovely bunch of coconuts.
There they are all standing in a row;
Big ones, small ones, some as big as . . .

At the exact moment that Her Majesty the Queen's horse sets foot on Horse Guards Parade in London the clock above the archway strikes eleven. It is never a minute late and certainly never early. This uncanny punctuality is put down to years of experience and to an elderly courtier who lives somewhere among the chimney pots and holds back the striker until the precise moment for the parade to begin.

It is possible to walk to Admiralty Arch along the rooftops from the Horse Guards. Early one morning in 1964, before the Queen's Birthday Parade was due to take place, security guards were alerted to a strange white flag flying above Admiralty Arch. It was a white cook's jacket and contained enough evidence, such as straw in a pocket and brass buttons, to implicate the Household Cavalry. A bored cook attached to the Queen's Life Guard had been 'sleep walking'. The relevant authority demanded stern retribution, but I could not help but sympathize with him and just reprimand him.

There are occasions of drama on that splendid parade which remain unknown to the public. There was a musician who fainted, but remained firmly in the saddle. The veterinary staff on duty noticed that his horse, now carrying a dead weight, had begun to sweat, so they withdrew both from the parade. And then there was the young ensign whose bearskin, unknown to him, contained a travelling alarm clock. It went off for fifteen seconds at eleven and nobody out of all those on parade could tell whose bearskin it was, because they were all saluting and facing the Queen.

No inspecting general should ever catch a Guard of Honour, however small, completely unprepared. Such an event was narrowly avoided when the driver of a visiting general's staff car stopped suddenly and engaged reverse the moment he saw that there was nobody outside the Guard Room. It was not the lack of Gurkha soldiers that made him realize he was early but their empty khaki shorts. Twelve pairs of starched, perfectly creased shorts were lined up on the road waiting for the cry 'Turn out the Guard'. The soldiers, running out of the Guard Room, might pause for a moment to step gingerly between the knife-edge creases before hoisting up their trousers and then 'present arms'. The immaculate soldiers were a credit to their battalion.

Whereas the parade on Horse Guards, with about 1,000 men taking part, is an impressive spectacle, much has been achieved with less. The late Brigadier George Butler, as a young officer stationed in Germany shortly after the war, was told to take three trucks to Belgium and load up with wine and other delicacies. On the return journey, he was not sure whether the *gendarmes* would allow his cargo to pass, so he lined up his six men and asked the head of the customs' post if he would do him the great honour of inspecting his men. The headquarter squadron drivers of the 8th Irish Hussars were not renowned for their smartness or military deportment, but they rose to the occasion. They smartened themselves up and put on a tremendous show, with cries of command, foot stamping, saluting and complicated arms drill. The senior *gendarme* then insisted that George should now inspect his men. George said he would be honoured to do so, but, as it was getting late, could the three trucks get going because they had a long way to go? He would follow in his jeep after the inspection. This was fully appreciated and agreed, much to George's relief.

Few ceremonies could equal the parade at the Officer Cadets' School, just outside Mexico City. This event was added during lunch to an already crowded programme. I was taking a party from the Royal College of Defence Studies in London to Canada, USA and South America. The Mexicans had already taken great pains to show us everything. After lunch the cadets were given twenty minutes to change into Full Dress, which was similar to German pre-1914 uniform, spiked helmets and black jackboots. Half-way up an Aztec pyramid there was a reviewing platform overlooking a parade

125

ground. Eight squadrons, 150 men each, marched past, goose-stepping with immaculate precision and dressing. The commander of each squadron carried a sword in his right hand and on his left wrist, close to his chest, an eagle. When they passed the saluting base the sword was brought down to the salute whilst the left arm was extended parallel to the ground and the eagles opened their wings. It was an amazing spectacle.

Things, of course, unexpectedly go wrong; words of command are forgotten and not even the good will of soldiers on parade will redeem the situation. In the late 1970s in West Berlin the British held their annual Queen's Birthday Parade in the old 1936 Olympic Stadium, a magnificent occasion, to which the Berliners flocked in their thousands. Three infantry battalions, massed bands, a cavalry squadron of tanks, helicopters and various other units were drawn up in lines on the Maifeld, where the only Olympic polo matches ever were held. At the close of the parade, when they all should have advanced in Review Order, the officer in command of the whole parade gave the wrong order. The line infantry showed indecision, the light infantry went off at the gallop, then stopped, and the Guards stood firm. Then Colonel Pielow, Chief of Staff, marched on to the parade and suggested to the mounted commander that he should look over his shoulder. The cry 'As You Were' soon restored the situation. The thousands of Berliners applauded at this evidence that we are, after all, only human and sometimes cannot help forgetting our lines.

This fear of forgetting words of command was overcome by Colonel Julian Berry when new standards were presented on Horse Guards to the Household Cavalry. He typed them on to a small piece of paper which he pasted to the inside of his white gauntlets, invisible to all but himself.

I had the good fortune to accompany General Sir Richard Gale, Deputy Supreme Allied Commander, Europe, on numerous trips around NATO. On one occasion we visited the Third Turkish Army Headquarters in Erzurum in Eastern Turkey. We flew in a twin-piston-engine Dakota, which, in deference to the VIPs it carried, had a carpet and a large green sofa instead of seats and safety belts. As we taxied along a rough runway towards a reception party, which included a band and a Guard of Honour, there was a violent lurch and the aircraft came to rest in an enormous pothole.

The reception party picked up their musical instruments, the red carpet, white ropes and fencing and began to double towards the stranded aircraft. Eventually, when they had all arrived, somewhat out of breath, some steps were set up against the aircraft door. The band struck up a march and the door opened to reveal the General, who took one look at the band, which contained a glockenspiel and gasped, 'My God, a Jingling Johnny. I must spend a penny,' and the door closed again. Eventually the ceremony concluded.

During the course of the next two days Gale must have promised that their bandmasters might enjoy a visit to London. Four of these gentlemen were eventually put up in the old Officers' Mess at Hyde Park Barracks. After two days, it seems, strange damage to the lavatories was noticed; not only did the cisterns leak but there were footmarks up the wall. Unaccustomed to our habits, it seems that the Turks preferred to stand on the china pedestal facing the wall, grab the down-pipe from the cistern with both hands and exert pressure with their feet on the wall.

Military ceremonial has been contrived to cover many contingencies, such as receiving the bones of airmen shot down over Berlin in the Second World War from the Russians to the handover of Hong Kong to the Republic of China, whose guard also performed a goose-step. In the United Kingdom Royal events such as the presentation of new Standards or Colours, amalgamations, change-of-command parades and ancient ceremonies like the Garter Parade at Windsor Castle, are all events which involve servicemen who have to stand still in rows. They should be thankful that they are not required to goosestep.

In Douala, in the Cameroons, I saw a much-neglected cracked memorial stone to the dead of four British ships who must have clashed with German warships in the First World War. Not far away, in the main street, was a gleaming white marble monument to the French army, surrounded by wreaths.

Placing a wreath on memorials to the war dead is a universal ceremony, but I was not prepared for what occurred in Jakarta, Indonesia. I was taken, with two Canadian officers, in a noisy cavalcade of sedan cars and military jeeps to the war graves outside the city. There I was given an old British steel helmet with a bullet-hole in it, which was filled with rose petals. Then, as I began to scatter them among the crosses, I realized that many of the graves might have been the result of the war with the British in Brunei!

There is an exception to this, which is the *kava* ceremony in Fiji. I was warned, before leaving Hong Kong, that it was terribly important to get my part of the ceremony right and cry out a word at the correct moment which sounded different every time someone tried to teach it to me. Unlike the *Haka* dance, designed to strike fear in the hearts of the enemies of New Zealanders, the Kava ceremony in Fiji was intended to calm down any visitors spoiling for a fight, put them into a pleasant stupor and impress them with such ceremonial and hospitality.

I was led to a large hangar where about 300 soldiers were sitting cross-legged in the shape of an open V, with a chair at the widest part for myself. Facing me, at the sharp end, was a giant of a man, stripped to the waist with huge throbbing muscles and a large wooden bowl with three legs between his knees. They then began a deep sonorous song a bit like a Gregorian chant which made the hair at the back of my neck tingle. An acolyte brought a yellow, twisted kava root to the big man who proceeded to scrunch it into pulp and drop it into the bowl. Two men appeared, carrying a bamboo log full of water slung from their shoulders, which they added to the yellow mess in the bowl. Men then appeared from all directions carrying fruits and vegetables which were dumped at my feet, including an entire cooked pig hanging from a pole. Then an important little man, possibly a witch doctor or maybe the adjutant (he looked familiar), approached the giant guarding the wooden bowl. He dipped half a coconut shell into the yellow liquid, came towards me with a disturbing glint in his eye, on his haunches. Then a great silence prevailed and I realized that the least I could do now was to say thank you for the bountiful feast and to give praise to the recent achievements of their soldiers. I also asked them to be so kind as to help me do justice to the magnificent feast because I could not possibly manage to do so alone. I was then handed the coconut shell, which I had been told to empty in one gulp. I had no idea whether it was hot, sweet, bitter or alcoholic, but I did so and remembered to uttered the word 'Bolla', or something similar. It was fortunate, I was told later, that I had invited them to enjoy the feast because an American four-star visitor had apparently said nothing and the whole lot, including the pig, had been dumped on his hotel bed. When I returned to my room I found a chocolate on my pillow and a message: 'Good night and pleasant dreams, Beatrice'. Some impulse, brought on no doubt by the *kava*'s hidden qualities, made me pull the bell rope. A gentle knock on the door and I was confronted by a very large lady indeed, heavy with twins and all smiles.

'Thank you for the sweet, Beatrice.'

PART V
1981–1996

Chapter 17

GREENLAND INUIT

Tell me, Father, what is the white man's heaven? Is it like the land of little trees when the ice has left the lake? Are the great musk oxen there? Are the hills covered with flowers? There, will I see the caribou everywhere I look? Are the lakes blue with the sky of summer? Is every net full of great, fat white fish? Is there room for me in this land, like our land the Barrens? Can I camp anywhere and not find that someone else has camped? Can I feel the wind and be like the wind? Father, if your heaven is not like all these, leave me alone in my land, the land of little sticks.

Dogrib Indian to Missionary

She was a brave little girl, crying with fear as she made her way downhill past a line of nine husky dogs, which lunged at her and bared their yellow fangs. They were each secured to a central wire rope by a chain, and if they came too close she bent down as if to pick up a stone. The dogs hesitated; then she ran a few steps and the dogs lunged again. She threw a rock, or pretended to; they stopped again and she ran until she was clear of the tethered dog team.

In late spring and summer, during which the ice, which covers the sea, has begun to melt, there are teams of huskies tethered in every vacant lot between the wooden houses. They stay there until the sea freezes solid again in September or October. The only animals allowed to roam are bitches with puppies less than three months old. In summer the dog teams are not exercised. They are only fed once every five days, because they are not burning up any energy. Woe betide anyone who falls within reach of those hungry jaws. No other animals are allowed in the settlement except for the Danish policeman's Alsatian hound.

I had reached Umanak in Greenland which clings to a tiny rocky island. It is dominated by a remarkable twin-peaked mountain, rising

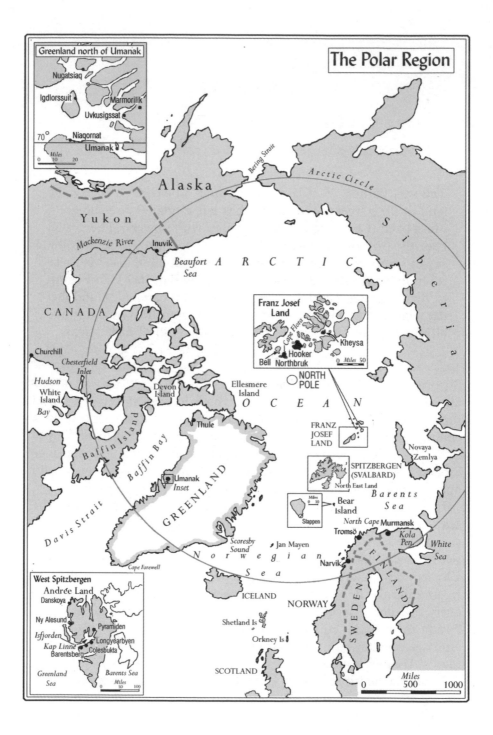

The Polar Region

Greenland north of Umanak
Nugatsiaq
Igdlorssuit
Marmorilik
Uvkusigssat
70°
Niaqornat
Umanak
Miles
0 10 20

Bering Strait
Arctic Circle
Alaska
Yukon
Mackenzie River
Inuvik
Beaufort
Sea
ARCTIC
Siberia
CANADA
Churchill
Chesterfield
Inlet
Hudson
White
Island
Bay
Devon
Island
Ellesmere
Island
OCEAN
Baffin Island
Baffin Bay
Thule
NORTH
POLE
Franz Josef
Land
Cape Flora
Kheysa
Hooker
Bell Northbruk
0 Miles 50
FRANZ
JOSEF
LAND
Novaya
Zemlya
SPITZBERGEN
(SVALBARD)
North East Land
Miles
0 10
Bear
Island
Stappen
Barents
Sea
Davis Strait
Umanak
Inset
GREENLAND
Scoresby
Sound
Jan Mayen
Norwegian
Sea
Cape Farewell
North Cape Murmansk
Tromsö
Narvik
Kola
Pen.
White
Sea
FINLAND
SWEDEN

West Spitzbergen
Andrée Land
Danskoya
Ny Alesund
Pyramiden
Isfjorden
Kap Linne
Longyearbyen
Barentsberg
Colesbukta
Greenland
Sea
Barents Sea
Miles
0 50 100

ICELAND
NORWAY
Shetland Is
Orkney Is
SCOTLAND
Miles
0 500 1000

sheer out of the pack ice. Seen from a distance, with a necklace of low cloud, it might hide an ideal site on which flying saucers choose to make a landing. Our Sikorsky helicopter swoops in, we jump out, grab our kit and start to walk round the mountain to the settlement. I was shown the government guesthouse and communal kitchen, dumped my rucksack on an empty wooden bunk and walked down to the harbour, a scene of much activity, because fishing boats, whalers and landing craft can only rely on the sea being free of ice in July and August. There are five weeks each side when the sea ice is either breaking up or freezing, making travel hazardous, or at least restricted. Midsummer is the time to offload timber and building materials for houses to be put together next summer. Many barrels of fuel oil are lined up on the shore beside every settlement and of course stocks of food and drink replenished before the long winter stops all travel by sea.

Greenland had been settled by Eskimo or Inuit people by at least 1000 BC. The Vikings arrived in AD 986, led by Erik the Red. The ruins of his house can still be seen in the far south. For some unknown reason Erik's descendants had all disappeared by about AD 1500. Perhaps the climate became a few degrees cooler and the crops failed. It was not until 1721 that Danish colonization began, with the arrival of Hans Egede, a missionary. The Danish government pays an annual subsidy to Greenland, which had increased to $300 million by 1980. In the north of Greenland nothing, neither fruit or vegetable, can grow. In theory nobody should starve because they can all draw on Denmark's generous Social Security. In practice much of this is treated as pocket money and is spent on cigarettes and drink.

During the Second World War the whole of Europe, less Switzerland, Sweden, Portugal and Britain, was occupied by the German Army. Denmark fell in a day. There had been no time in which to set up a government in exile. There seemed to be no way that the Danish colony in Greenland and the Inuit population could be sustained. Without any guidance from Copenhagen, the Danish Ambassador in Washington made a personal deal with the USA. He agreed to allow the USA to build air bases at Thule in the north-west of Greenland and at Stromfjord in the south-west in exchange for the USA providing food and fuel for the people of Greenland until the war ended.

135

Meanwhile, the Danish police and Inuit volunteers, assisted by the US Coastguards, waged a lonely war against the Germans.

There are about 44,000 Greenlanders, a people of Eskimo descent, and about 10,000 foreigners, mainly Danish. This huge country has a coastline as long as the distance from the Shetland Islands to Gibraltar. About 11,000 people live in Gothab, the capital, the rest live in sixteen very small 'towns' and in sixty tiny settlements. None, I believe, are linked to each other or indeed could possibly be, because the distances are immense and the terrain impassable. However, in some towns there are a few kilometres of rocky road, along which tractors and a few four-wheel-drive cars move in low gear. Winter, when the sea is frozen, is the time to go visiting. Every household seems to have a dog team. The seventy tons of dog mess dumped onto the streets of London each day is nothing compared to the mess that piles up outside a Greenland home. Nothing gets swept up; when the dogs are hungry they will eat anything. After months of inactivity, there is joy when the snow covers up the dog mess and the huskies can be harnessed to a sled. They have right of way and move silently and swiftly. Pedestrians in the settlements have to be alert and nimble to keep out of their way.

I was offered a trip to Niaqormat where my friend Konrad Rauschenberger wished to inspect a water catchment system he had constructed a few years before. We set off in a motor launch from Umanak on a sea as calm as a mirror. There were some large icebergs glistening in the sunlight, cast into strange shapes. We had been sailing for an hour when, quite suddenly, thick fog descended and we couldn't see more than 2 metres. The skipper stopped the engines and we all strained our eyes, when suddenly, towering above our little boat, was the first iceberg I had actually met. It was quite unexpected and frightening. We hit it gently and pushed the boat clear. The fog lifted as quickly as it descended and in the distance I could see our destination. It was going to be a dry landing; the village had a wooden pier on which five Inuit ladies, wearing brightly coloured anoraks, sat smoking. The settlement was on a narrow spit of land between two cliffs of red rock. There were two very old houses built from rocks and turf and four solid houses built from the heavy timbers of the old whaling ships. The rest of the houses had been built from soft wood and painted in bright colours. They stood on pillars of different heights because the ground is seldom level and air must be left between the floor and the ground if the heat of the dwelling is not to thaw the frozen topsoil.

Steps had been cut in the red rock leading to a plateau from which I could look down on the village. It had been quite a climb and I realized the symbolism, because on the plateau is the cemetery. Lugging the departed up all those steps, way above the roofs, must have given them a headstart on the way to heaven. Like all graves in the High Arctic, it is not possible to dig a hole, so bodies are covered with heavy rocks in order to prevent wild animals disturbing the burial. Graves are not always in the cemetery. I saw a pile of rocks, a skull, bones and a boot about half a mile inland, high above a track with a magnificent view of the village and icebergs.

The villagers had built a long wooden frame on which fish and seal skins had been nailed to dry. Among the skins there was one of an old husky dog which, I was unhappy to learn, was hanged so that it would die of fright, its fur standing on end.

Sitting on a dog sled in winter can be terribly cold. Skins are used to make outer clothing and sleeping bags. Polar bear skin has long hair and husky dog hair is very coarse; both tend to moult and hair gets into the stew. Caribou and reindeer hair is short and brittle and least noticeable when blown into the food, a little like parmesan cheese on spaghetti I am told.

Next day we set sail for Igdlorssuit on a tiny schooner with a crew of four swarthy, dark Inuit. We chugged carefully through a sea of broken bits of pack ice and a few small icebergs. One of the crew who had been dozing on the wheelhouse roof spotted a seal. Suddenly the deck became like a scene from a Western as the crew took up their rusty Lee Enfield and Mauser rifles and started shooting. In the middle of the ensuing fusillade an 'Eskimo Nell', who I did not know was on board, appeared from the crew's quarters making strange excited war cries and brandishing a gun. She had to be restrained and told to calm down. Her brother, two days previously, had murdered her husband and she had come along for the ride because she felt she needed a change of scene and some quiet!

Unless the first snap shot hits the seal it will dive and stay hidden for up to ten minutes until it has to come up for air, usually in a completely different place. If the second shot is swift, but again misses, the seal has less time to take a deep breath, so will only be able to stay under for five minutes. The time spent under water gets progressively less and a wise seal will by now have swum sideways and taken shelter behind a friendly iceberg.

About 200 killometres north of Umanak we reached the settlement of Nûgâtsiaq. In a tiny bay the traditional Inuit kayak seemed to have been replaced by orange plastic boats with outboard motors. Looking down into the boats, they all seem to carry, in addition to fishing tackle, some of the rustiest rifles I have ever seen. There is always the hope that a seal or an eider duck will be shot on a fishing trip. Pragmatically, no life jackets are carried because the Inuit cannot swim. What is the point when the icy water will kill you anyway?

There was a dump of empty oil barrels waiting to be refilled. I set up my shaving mirror and towel and found myself surrounded by children in bright jackets. They examined the contents of my rucksack; I thanked heaven that at least my dentures were in my mouth! Outside every house (there are only nine) hung an array of skins, fish, birds and drying laundry. They do the laundry in half a bucket of water and it freezes solid in minutes. After a week it is completely dehydrated and beautifully soft. If clothing is brought inside when it is frozen stiff and knocks against a table or door, it shatters like glass and you discover that you have lost an arm and a shirt tail!

I made friends with a Dane who was sitting in the morning sunshine outside his house mending a fishing net. He was married to an Inuit. He invited me into his home, furnished in a simple but practical way. There was a kitchen of sorts and a sink unit. There was no running water, but every house kept a large plastic dustbin just inside the door. Lumps of ice, which drift onto the shore, are broken up and carried indoors in plastic bags. This ice is thousands of years old, absolutely free from acid rain or nuclear fallout, part of the Greenland icecap. The closet is a bucket containing a plastic bag, often overfull, which is allowed to freeze outside and then carried some distance away from the village. There are wooden shelves, a table, chairs and the one typically Inuit piece of furniture, a low platform bigger than a double bed which is used for everything from sewing to sleeping. The living room had curtains and lino on the floor. The walls were covered with faded photographs and magazine pictures. A few decorative plates and plastic flowers reminded the poor chap of home. He fetched two cans of beer and invited me to join him. His wife remained on her knees on the floor scraping the flesh from a sealskin with a curved blade.

He explained that the only way he can make any money for essentials is by hunting seal and selling the skins. The activities of organizations like Green Peace very nearly brought starvation to the settlement, because so few seals could be killed. He explained that it could sometimes take a whole day to stalk, kill and recover a seal.

When Denmark recovered Greenland after the Second World War the people were in terrible shape. They were ravaged by epidemics, measles in 1931, followed by polio in 1953. Venereal disease was first noticed in 1910, having been brought in by sailors from whaling fleets. In 1968 there were 6,168 cases of VD, mainly gonorrhoea. By 1986 this had risen to over 12,000 cases and now one in four adults has VD. The birth rate has soared and so has child mortality. The problem is that the Inuit are a very friendly and accommodating people. They may not have the same sensuous grace one might associate with a South Sea Island maiden. Their hospitality, however, is natural and not always linked to their promiscuity. Nevertheless, when a visitor from a distant village arrives in midwinter, and there are no newspapers, no books, no radio and no electricity because the generator is broken or fuel is short, what else is there to do? It has been said that Japanese tourists thought that Greenland might be another Thailand but were soon put off by the high risk of catching VD.

I spotted a faded picture on the wall of a tall European towering over an Inuit, both in Inuit ceremonial dress. It was of their wedding eighteen years ago. The Dane had been trained in plating, especially chrome, but found a course he attended in Britain too difficult. He then served in the Danish Navy before coming to Greenland. The unexpectedly hard life had shrunken him and he had nearly starved. His three children were all in great heart; his wife smoked a pack of cigarettes and he drank about two cans of beer a day. His cans were among the very few which ended up in a trash bin.

I left his wife still scraping away, little bits of flesh, hair and blood all over the place. Thank heavens for lino, which is washable. I noticed that the number of his house was 1203, which did not tally with the dozen or so houses which make up the village. He explained that in Umanak district houses are numbered in the order they were erected, irrespective of where they are situated. Thus a newly built school house and a new fish store will have consecutive numbers even though they are 200 miles apart. During the 1960s each village was given a small block of numbers and told to number their homes. They took great care to choose numbers that looked attractive. Houses which had been standing next to each other for over fifty years were nevertheless given random lucky numbers. As there is no postal service to the settlements the puzzled Inuit will never see what is the point of giving a house a number except as a decorative status symbol.

Igdlorsuiit is the most miserable village I have ever seen. It seemed that the sun seldom shines on the village, which was strung out along a beach of black sand. There are no sea shells or any sign of marine life. The dirt and litter are indescribable. I rowed ashore in a dinghy loaded with about thirty-five different packages, all of which had to be lugged up to a government resthouse. The door to this wooden hut is unlocked by a tedious lady who knows five words of English which she keeps repeating: 'I fuck good; try me'. She keeps popping in, and then gets terribly drunk on the dregs from a number of wine bottles which stand on the floor beside the door. She knocks her glass over and buries her head in her hands. What a mess! I feel sorry for her because, I am told, her husband shot himself two weeks ago over a much younger girl.

The village seemed to have no spark and the dogs wandered about loose, defecating outside every house. The hinterland is barren and hard to reach, but at least the cemetery was surrounded by a neat white fence, which keeps the dogs out. A little higher on the hill are the rock cairns and marker stones of a much older burial ground. I walked back along the foreshore until I saw a group of ladies gutting halibut which had been caught on a baited hook. With an easy movement they slit the fish and flick the innards into the sea which turns pink, to be washed away by the five-foot tide. A rope was then threaded through the gills and the fish strung out to dry with the laundry. There are other fish, which I saw in Umanak; these are bright red and are caught very deep below the surface. When brought to the surface their eyes pop out like huge bubbles. The predominant colour of the laundry seems to be pink, which I take must be due to the dye running, not blood.

There must have been close on 200 dogs all howling at once. The filth between the debris of half-built houses is indescribable. Inside the resthouse the Elsan bucket is full up to 2 centimetres from the top. It is going to take a steady hand to carry it out of the house.

There is no clean water except a little pool on the far side of a swamp and well clear of the loose huskies.

Our departure was delayed because the vessel has been holed. We had anchored in the lee of a small island; then the wind intensified and changed 180 degrees, so we pulled the boat higher up the shore. However, an iceberg broke and fell into the water with a crash, causing a small tidal wave, which lifted the boat and holed it on a small rock. We were happy that an Inuit plumber and his Danish wife offered us a lift in his fast launch to the village of Uvkusigssat. We set off late, provisions to be transshipped before Konrad, Minna (our interpreter) and Niels, a Danish administrator, came on board. We had barely begun to thread our way through a cluster of small icebergs when strange noises and smoke started to come out of the engine. The plumber had forgotten to open the stopcock to allow the seawater to cool the engine. We were towed back and three hours later set off once more; it was now 8 pm and broad daylight.

It was a fantastic trip, weaving in between icebergs at 15 knots. We paused to look at a glacier flowing into the sea. About 100 feet above the waterline on the scree two skis had been erected as a memorial to two Italian climbers who were killed the previous year. A ring of stone round the site had been painted red, white and green, the Italian colours. Then suddenly we plunged deep into fog. It was an alarming experience. There were icebergs and no radar. The plumber had set the compass allowing 51 degrees out of True North because we were so close to the Magnetic Pole. He soon had no idea where we were. After two and a half hours and no landfall he realized that something was wrong. Eventually we saw the coastline and followed it until the plumber saw a landmark, where he did an about-turn. There was no foghorn or any navigation lights. Some time after 1 am we reached the little jetty at Uvkusigssat. It was still broad daylight and about thirty people had turned out to greet us. It was such a relief to carry our kit ashore and to head for the new schoolhouse where we slept on the highly polished floor.

Down by the jetty was an old stone and turf house which had a huge yellow K 13 painted on its roof. This was a relic of the Second World War and every major settlement had one house on the water's edge marked with a similar identification sign on its roof. Aircraft were being flown to England from America via Canada, Newfoundland, Greenland, Iceland and Scotland. The pilots were untrained and hopeless at navigation. They were told, on leaving Gander, to fly due east until they saw land which could only be Greenland. Then they should turn right (south) until they flew over a village and compare the number on the roof with their key map. It was so simple that they should have no difficulty in finding and landing at Stromfjord in Greenland. Of course it did not always work out and a four-engine B26 bomber and six Mustang fighters made a forced landing in 1944 on the inaccessible Greenland icecap. A miraculous rescue took place and the aircraft, which are still there, have sunk at least 30 metres under the ice.

Uvkusigssat is built on a rocky slope which rises straight out of the sea. This village seemed to have more self-respect than other settlements. Every house had been painted a bright colour. The headman apologized that there was still one house unpainted; did we have any ideas what colour it should be? We decided on a warm shade of yellow.

There was to be a christening the next day, an occasion to which Minna had been invited. Minna had been married to a Dane who died of tuberculosis before they could start a family. She had a sweet face, which, when she was alone, looked terribly sad. Two men dressed in white suits came to collect her; maybe one was the priest, as he wore a sash and a smock. I watched the party process up through the village past a dead dog whose body I was told would not be removed until Monday. But today was Sunday and the cheerful villagers piled into boats to join villagers from a nearby village, Marmorilik, to go on a fishing trip. They were then going to join the christening party which was not expected to finish before lunch the next day.

I sat down on a pile of planks with the schoolmaster and watched their departure. He was a most interesting person. I took the chance to ask him what had happened to Greenland during in the War. Greenland had never been a theatre of war before, but, although very little happened, it nevertheless was to have a significant bearing on the plans of both sides. The prize was accurate weather forecasts. Weather stations were located high in the Arctic in Greenland, in Jan Mayen Island and Spitzbergen. Before the war these had been manned by Danes and Norwegians. Now the stations had been withdrawn or destroyed. There was no longer a source of accurate weather information on which every bombing raid and every major military attack in Northern Europe depended. The Allied landings in France and Italy, the escape of German battleships up the channel, the defeat of the German Ardennes offensive, every major river crossing, are examples of the value of weather forecasts. Very soon the Germans were setting up secret weather stations in remote locations on the east coast of Greenland.

The Danish governor of Greenland, Eske Brun, a civil servant, realized that, with his country occupied by the Nazis, all orders from Copenhagen must inevitably have been sent under duress. How could he possibly defend Greenland? In a population of about 20,000 there was nobody who had ever received any military training. The Americans had set up a few bases in the west and south, but the east coast was unprotected. Eske Brun took the advice of the Americans and ordered everyone living north of Scoresby Sound to move south.

Living in this vast, inhospitable area there were only twenty-four men and one woman, half were Danish or Norwegian trappers and half were Inuit or Danish policemen. Thus it was that the 'Greenland sled patrol' was created. Their mission was to patrol with dogs as far as 77° North, beyond which the sea stayed frozen all year. In 1943 they discovered that the Germans were already on Greenland and operating their own weather station. This was found by a sled patrol led by a policeman called Jensen, and two Inuit, William and Mikael. They were, however, surprised as they slept by Germans and only just escaped, while their dogs attacked the strangers. They had no time to harness the dogs. Jensen told the Inuit to get to their base at Eskimonaes and to warn the authorities that the enemy were already on Greenland, but he stayed to watch what the Germans did, though he soon had to get moving because he had no outer clothing or footwear. It is quite amazing that Jensen, wearing insufficient clothes and without food, managed to stagger 50 miles in the bitter cold. The schoolmaster told me, with some pride, that he was related to Jensen, who had an even more remarkable escape a few weeks later.

It seems that the Germans were commanded by one Lieutenant Herman Ritter, an Austrian, who before the war had lived for five years with his wife as a trapper in Spitzbergen. He now ambushed three sled patrols. He had ordered his men not to kill the Danes or Inuit, but to kill the dogs. The first sled to arrive was driven by a man called Knudsen, who had been one of the twelve trappers ordered to move south. The Germans had already opened fire when Ritter shouted, 'The dogs, the dogs'. Some of the dogs were hit, but so too was Knudsen, who became the first and only Greenlander to be killed during the war. Two more sleds were captured, one driven by Jensen and one by a man called Nielson.

The Germans now had several dog teams, but nobody was able to harness or control them. The Danes refused to train the Germans. Ritter realized his presence must now be known and that the Americans would find them and bomb them, so he split his force. He allowed Nielson to go and build Knudsen a proper burial cairn. He was then to wait until Ritter's men collected him. Jensen, however, knew that once the work was complete Nielson would escape.

Ritter sent his men to a secret German base at Hansa Bay and for some inexplicable reason set off alone with Jensen by a different route. On the way Ritter got careless and Jensen was able to turn the tables and seize his rifle. That night, when they halted beside a hunting hut at Mosquito Bay, Jensen unloaded Ritter's sleeping bag, took some food and then drove the sled out of sight, saying he would be back in a few days. He knew that Ritter had no idea where he was and could not escape. He then settled down to a short sleep before hurrying south to Scoresby Sound where he warned his commander of the German presence. Jensen now retraced his steps for over 100 miles to Mosquito Bay. He could have forgotten about Ritter, but such is the humanitarian code of the Arctic that he could never have left him without the means to defend himself from polar bears. The danger of meeting other German patrols was great and Jensen drove his dogs as hard as he could for the next three days to Scoresby Sound.

The schoolmaster explained that, because the sled patrols were not enlisted soldiers, they were not protected by the Geneva Convention. If captured as civilians they could have been executed by the Germans. They were all made officers or non-commissioned officers in the Danish Army. The Germans continued to look for suitable places for their weather stations in Eastern Greenland and lost a number of ships in the ice and from attacks by US aircraft. They even tried automatic weather-forecast stations, but these seldom worked for more than two weeks before the batteries ran out.

I returned to the new school building, unpacked my things and made a pillow from my rucksack. It had been a long day and I soon fell asleep. Sometime later I felt the zip on my sleeping bag being undone and a hand cautiously feeling round my chest down to my underpants. I opened my eyes to see the bare upper half of an Inuit lady. I remembered reading that, when first discovered by white men, some Inuit mothers developed multiple breasts. This was on account of the very harsh, long winters and the need to suckle their children for up to three years. I opened my eyes wider and carried out a stock check. She only had two breasts and from their unaccustomed odour I took it that they had not been exposed to the air for a week or so. She made her demands clear and added that she would like some whisky. I was well aware that one in four of her countryfolk had some form of sexual disease. I had no wish to hurt her feelings, so I gave her a bottle of export-strength single malt and told her that I was going for a walk.

I picked my way through the dogs' mess, plastic bags, beer cans and shallow pools of stagnant water and sat on a sled. What on earth was the attraction of living in this bleak settlement at the base of a snow-covered mountain? It was probably the good fishing and seal hunting. I walked up through the village, past the rusty oil drums until I got well clear of the houses and could look down on the harbour and bay. Somewhere below, the eerie wolf-like howl of a husky was joined by every other dog in the village. This melancholy midnight chorus reached a crescendo and suddenly died away. Perhaps this was no worse than living under the flight path to London airport. It was still daylight, the sun would not set tonight. A deep boom rumbled up from the calm waters of the bay. The top of an iceberg had crashed into the sea and the following wave lifted some boats dangerously high before bringing them down close to the rocks. Two Inuit boys, who had been kicking a black and white football against a rock, stopped to stare down at three whales which surfaced from time to time and blew jets of water into the air, making a hissing sound. It was beautiful, pure magic.

Reluctantly I returned to the school house, wondering how on earth I could get rid of Eskimo Nell without a lot of noise. Mercifully she had passed out and had only drunk half the bottle. With the help of the Danish administrator, I carried her into another room and locked the door. As I drifted into an uneasy sleep the huskies began to howl once more.

Chapter 18

THE GENERAL

It had been a bad week for the General. The Soviet Union was having a power struggle with the Chinese about the former's North-Eastern frontiers. As a token of their support for Russia, all the Soviet satellite countries had agreed to shun their Chinese colleagues at receptions in both East and West Berlin. General Li, Chinese defence attaché, stood all alone in a corner, watching those lucky enough to be on the Allied Protocol list circulate around him. Berlin had been left in a time warp since the Second World War ended in 1945. All those countries which had been our Allies remained our friends, even though some were now openly hostile to the West. They received ration cards allowing them to buy their wine and spirits at that essentially British emporium, the NAAFI shop. Indeed the only effective sanction if they misbehaved in our sector of Berlin was to withdraw their NAAFI cards. The protocol list included about seventy Consuls and honorary Consuls, mostly German businessmen, who also wanted access to our whisky.

General Li was taller than most Chinese, with high cheek bones and a sense of humour, or, as my wife pointed out, at least he laughed at my jokes. As a young boy he had accompanied his father on 'the long march', until the Communists began to take control of mainland China in 1946. It was at the third such official reception in one week that I suggested to him how much more pleasant it would be if we could sit down and enjoy a cup of excellent China tea at my house, the Villa Lemm. This was an enchanting 'ginger-bread house' with pointed roofs and painted shutters and gardens running down to the Havel, a waterway running through the heart of West Berlin. To my surprise he agreed.

The first time he came with an interpreter. I thought I would break the ice by showing him round the garden. I called to the wild duck sitting on the Havel. They took off noisily and landed at our feet. Li

146

knew a lot about ducks, as I should have realized, and he took special interest in the drake, who had a limp. Our German cook, Peter, had tried to get it to follow a trail right into the kitchen. Furious that it would not hang around to be slaughtered, he had flung a knife at it, hence the limp. Now, three years later, it was the first to arrive but often last to reach the food.

At those meetings, each of us with a staff officer present, we discussed international events, warily sounding out each other's position. Then he casually asked whether we knew anything about the new Russian battle tank. His face lit up when I said yes and showed him a photograph. Like carrying out business in a bazaar, he then told me about special Russian forces who spoke English or other NATO languages, dressed in NATO uniforms and drove, for example, Land Rover cars. Their mission was to disrupt our command system. This was exactly what the German Army in the 1944 break through the American lines did, or threatened to do. The result was that the Allied Commander-in-Chief, General Eisenhower, was so worried by the threat of assassination that at the height of that crucial battle he hid in a room in Paris for six days, completely out of touch with his troops.

Meetings with General Li were often fruitful and continued to take place until I received a posting order to leave Berlin six months early and move to Hong Kong to become Commander, British Forces.

So I parted with General Li who said, 'Who knows? We might meet again.' Little did I realize what that first cup of China tea would lead to.

There was to be no further meeting with General Li once I left Berlin for Hong Kong. However, while I was away in Brunei visiting a Gurkha battalion, a Chinese businessman called at my house (Headquarter House on the Peak) and handed a letter to Valerie, my wife. His name was 'Buster' Chung and the message was that General Li sent greetings and invited us to be his guests in China. We would have loved to accept, but the Governor and his Foreign Office political advisor were appalled and vetoed the idea.

Even my request that we should be allowed to visit China after my retirement from the Army and only spend a few hours in Hong Kong on our return so as to catch the regular Royal Air Force flight back to England, to which we were entitled, was declined.

So that was that. I left the Army to become Director General of the Winston Churchill Memorial Trust. Three years later a Mr Brown, from MI6, who I had known in Berlin, invited me to lunch at the Royal Commonwealth Society. I recall that he ordered an unusual bottle of wine from a vineyard in Lamberhurst, Kent. He then explained that they had received reports from various overseas stations that the Chinese had been making enquires about me. Would I consider a visit to China with my wife, all expenses paid, except travel to China, 'in order to open a new hotel, *The Fragrant Hill*, near Beijing'? Brown added that his department would be very interested if such a visit took place and encouraged me to accept. I wrote afterwards to the Director of Security, seeking clearance, saying, 'I did hope that once I had retired and left Hong Kong my contact with Li would be past history'.

At our next meeting, in my home in Chelsea, which Valerie and my son Alexander attended, Mr Brown introduced Mr Watson, who was to be my link with MI6. They briefed me and stressed that it would be of considerable interest to them if I went to China. However, there was one snag. Because I was no longer a serving officer their department could not pay for the travel. Did I still wish to go? I was not going to miss this chance of a lifetime. There would never be another invitation, so I agreed to go, but reluctantly conceded that I could not possibly pay for two tickets at over £1,000 each. Mr Watson came to see me again in order to discuss the itinerary which I had received from 'Buster' Chung by air mail from Hong Kong.

The aircraft was, not surprisingly, full of Chinese except for a spotty young lady called Shirley, who was a courier for a travel firm in Croydon, and a Nigerian doctor who somehow managed to sleep throughout the hideous twenty-two hour flight. The air hostesses wore shapeless blue trouser suits and big happy smiles. The food was awful, washed down with lots of orange juice. I was met by General Li, his wife, a 'cousin' and 'Buster' Chung. They had been waiting at what seemed to be a deserted airport for four hours; we had been held up by fog at Dubai. 'Buster' led me to a VIP lounge, bypassing customs and immigration controls. While he found my suitcase, General Li explained that the *Fragrant Hill Hotel* had been opened a week earlier, causing terrible congestion, and how fortunate I was to come now, thus neatly disposing of the cover story and the reason for their invitation. I was relieved to discover that Mrs Li spoke a little English.

We climbed into an enormous black sedan called a 'Red Flag' and drove for one and a half hours through the capital and into the countryside. We passed through wide, dimly lit streets, deserted except for countless bicycles with no lights. General Li told me that Jackie Kennedy and her new husband had come to the opening of the *Fragrant Hill,* and a gentleman called Dale Keller, a renowned interior architect who had designed part of the hotel. We had dinner in a private room: crinkly white tree fungus soup, which was excellent, sea cucumber and more fungus, followed by a large freshwater fish which might have been carp, covered in hot, spicy breadcrumb and nut sauce, with a glass of Chinese red wine, which resembled medium sweet sherry.

During dinner Li began to ask questions. Why had permission to meet him not been granted by the Governor four years ago? What sort of chap was the political advisor? Why was he against our meeting? What was the difference between my job in Hong Kong and that in Berlin? How often did I meet the Russians in Berlin? I mentioned that the British Ambassador, Sir Percy Cradock, whom I had known in Berlin, had offered me lunch. Li seemed somewhat put out, but said of course it was only courtesy that I should go; adjustments would be made to the programme. In the event I did not visit the British Embassy and they all seemed much relieved.

The bedroom I was given was a corner suite, huge, four rooms in all, but not a single wardrobe or cupboard. I was too tired to look for the microphones and cameras I felt sure were trained onto my pillow. Next day 'Buster' proudly showed me round. There was clearly still much to complete. The dining room had been designed so that eight long tables were placed to enjoy the view from eight tall windows. The dining chairs had, however, been manufactured 5 centimetres too wide so that no waiter, however supple or thin, could pass between.

We then walked up a hill to a small temple with Li and his wife. Li asked many questions about the Winston Churchill Memorial Trust of which I was Director General. To what sort of people did we give fellowships, in what countries, what subjects? What would I do when I retired? Would I consider a business with 'Buster' Chung? I explained that I was already retired. We stopped several times while

149

he fired more questions. Did I still have military contacts? No, I was completely out of touch, but I had personal friends. What sort of reports did Churchill Fellows write? Did they go to the Government? No, they were not secret and of no military value. Would I like to be the London end of a family business in Beijing and Hong Kong? Maybe, if I sent an invitation, Li could visit London. Why had it been politically difficult to make my visit? I said because I had to get permission from the Trustees of the WCMT, the security services and because of Mrs Thatcher's visit to China.

The questioning continued and it was clear that every word I had written or spoken to him had been analysed and was then thrown back at me if there were any doubts. It took days to come to a point and many questions were just double-checking on my previous remarks. I began to realize that I was very much on my own and, if things turned sour, I would have no support from London.

We descended the hill and climbed into the 'Red Flag' limousine. Curiously, the number plate, I noted, was 007! The car was very heavy, possibly armour-plated, with very sluggish acceleration. The rear windows had brown curtains, which all but prevented anyone seeing in or out. We drove to the Summer Palace, a beautiful place set in gardens on Longevity Hill, and Peaceful Lake, on which the lotus plants had dried out. We met General Li's charming sons, one aged nineteen, just starting in a newspaper office and the other twenty-seven, a gaunt hungry boy, a captain in the Army, who had fought against the Vietnamese. We had tea beside the Sleeping Buddha, where the boys kept rushing off to bring more pots of tea.

The soldier son told me that they were poorly equipped in Vietnam; he only had his uniform and a raincoat; there were no tents or buildings in which to shelter. Now he started work at 6 am and had to study in the evenings. He was engaged to a most attractive doctor, aged twenty-six. She told me that her dream was one day to have a bedroom all to herself. I felt so sorry for her.

Then we all piled into the car and were taken to see the new hotel. Parties of 'Workers' had also arrived and were being shown round the dining room and the bedrooms. I went to find the bar which was in the care of two delightful young men who had never stood behind a bar before. For the next hour I tried to explain to them the basic difference between gin and whisky, between a liqueur and a sherry

150

and so on. I said that they had to taste everything once, so as to know what it was. The session ended in fits of Chinese giggles.

Next day I moved into the city, room 3015 in the Beijing Hotel. Each floor in a Chinese hotel has an attendant who takes your key whenever you leave the room. Chinese breakfast was from a choice of about twenty-five dishes, mainly rice gruel and bean curd. The bread was very heavy dough, but I managed to find a cup of coffee.

We set off at 7 am for the Great Wall. The city was like a building site. Mile after mile of houses were being built, using no machinery, and piles of small narrow bricks, like the Romans. There were hundreds of workers with shovels and wheelbarrows. At every red traffic light there were at least twenty bicycles abreast. We passed green military-looking trucks with people standing in the back looking out over the driver's cab. There were motor-cycles with side-cars, columns of horse-drawn carts and three-wheeled tractors drawing trailers piled high with goods to sell in the market. I counted twenty separate flocks of sheep and their shepherds, with sleeping bags draped round their shoulders. They must have come down from the mountains because the valley was brown and scorched. There were no sheep dogs, but then no cats or dogs are allowed in the capital; even the size of a Chinese family is limited to one child; the law insists that the others are aborted.

The Wall is 78 miles from Beijing. We drove through hills and scrub, which I could only see clearly if I held back the brown curtains which hid the back of the car. We arrived early in the day, but shortly afterwards busloads of Chinese tourists joined us. A sea of humanity began to gasp its way up towards one of the watch towers. Local photographers did a roaring trade, taking pictures of people sitting on a camel with two humps. There were patient queues waiting for the negatives to be processed in a bucket of developing fluid and then hung to dry on a clothes line. Western and Japanese tourists, who had their own cameras, looked on in amazement. It soon became apparent that the Japanese were unpopular. As I was climbing the steps we met, 'quite by chance', a little round man who had been a classmate of General Li. He was fifty-one years old and had been military attaché in Prague. He spoke Russian, Czech and English. I was allowed to photograph him. We chatted and he asked if I had ever met Mrs Thatcher, which I had not. He said she was so nervous that she even forgot to shake the hand of her host, the Chinese

Foreign Minister. Had I seen the television pictures of it? They had showed it there twice, in slow motion.

I said goodbye to him and we drove to the Ming Tombs, which are approached along an avenue of stone statues of animals and soldiers. There are thirteen Ming Tombs visible, but only one has been examined. It took years to discover the secret of how to open the solid white marble doors, all interlocked by more blocks set at angles in the walls. The contents were remarkable gold and silver objects, brilliant blue storage jars holding wine, oil and rice, and wooden gilt furniture.

On the way Li told me that, as a General, his uniform was now made of better material and his house was free. On retirement he would be given a car. His pension was calculated from the day he joined, aged eleven, in 1938. He received an extra month's pay a year, paid no tax and might be allowed to retain his driver. He was anxious to know what I got. I told him and he was not impressed, but then neither am I. We had lunch in the Beihai Park at the Peking Duck Restaurant where 'Buster' aired his ideas on what sort of business we might run: special Chinese items for Chinese restaurants in the West, crockery, sauces, a Do-it-Yourself shop using Chinese-made tools which were very cheap. General Li surprised me by saying that many Pakistani Generals had another job 'on the side', because they were so poorly paid. He said that the address I was meant to make to their Institute of Strategic Studies had been cancelled because I did not have a speech ready. That I should even attend such an event was news to me and suggests that, in the daily inspection of my belongings in my room, they could not find a draft. Li added, 'Don't worry. My superior will see you and you can then tell him what you would have told the Institute. We are having dinner with him afterwards.' I wrote in my pocket diary, 'The crunch cometh'.

The next day we visited the Forbidden City, in the heart of Beijing. There was a huge collection of carriage clocks, including a water clock. These were ornate and covered in jewels manufactured for the Chinese market, possibly in Britain, but more likely made in Hong Kong or India. Several had automated scenes which had human and animal figures which moved every hour.

Lunch was in a private room in Pai Hai Park, 'very hard to get'. The manager stood kowtowing at the door. He explained that cooks, who had been trained by the 'last Chinese Empress', had prepared our lunch and that the skills had been handed down through three generations. They made some exceptionally good sweets, containing almonds and quince fudge. Taking advantage of being allowed to use the government entertainment funds, Li's soldier son and his fiancée, called Ping, joined us. She was in her last month at medical school and specialized in throat and cell biology. I made a note that she would love to have a book on the subject in English. I never found one.

Li invited me to visit the National Army Museum. This, it seems, was a privilege for a Westerner and was confirmed by the fact that there were no other Westerners in the building, guarded by two smart sentries. There was a definite anti-American slant to the collection. Several interesting displays concerned the early use of gunpowder and rocket-propelled arrows. Many rooms showed the war against Japan of 1937 and the civil war against Chiang Kai-shek. Many maps and blown-up pictures filled four of the rooms.

Li then said, 'And now I shall show you a captured British tank.'

I replied, 'We never lost a single tank in Korea.' So he took me to an enormous hangar full of armoured fighting vehicles. There were twenty-three American tanks and a British-made Bren-gun carrier with a Canadian maple leaf sign.

'That is not a tank,' I pointed out with relief.

Suspended from the ceiling were various American aircraft, including a complete black U2. Somewhat crumpled, but nevertheless most impressive with its colossal wingspan. 'We shot down four,' said General Li. I was indeed impressed.

Then I was taken to meet Li's boss in the government hospitality building, which may once have been an embassy. Two smart sentries stood at the entrance and three officials appeared as soon as my foot touched the ground. We went up the steps of a grand porch and were ushered into a large room with five double windows along one side. There were eight sofas around the walls and a splendid red carpet. We were ushered to the far end of the salon where I was introduced to my host, Mr Chang. There was a small, cheerful, old interpreter and a member of staff who took notes. Li and his wife sat very much on the edge of their chairs; she helped with translations from time to time.

Mr Chang, it seemed, came from the same village as Li and was about 65 years old; he had a son who was an engineer, and a daughter. Our preliminary chat covered England, children, cooking, gardens and ancient monuments. Then he switched to serious matters. Although the West might imagine that China and the Soviet Union were making friends again, this was not so. Brezhnev was no dove. Russian hegemony continued and he detailed Russian expansion into Africa and the wars they had started. He stressed that Brezhnev had been expanding worldwide and would continue to do so. I asked him who might succeed Brezhnev and what changes should we expect. He said that he envisaged no changes and that Brezhnev's successor might be the head of the KGB, or Gorpodov, a name I could not get. The Russians are very chauvinistic, he told me; national minorities are all being suppressed, Germans, Jews and other races. In the view of the Chinese, Russians are not true Marxists. The Kremlin might fall only if there are forces within which can 'purify Russian politics', or because of outside pressure building up, for instance in Eastern Europe. No external force could bring about a change. It was not the intention of the Chinese to attack Russia. There was no evidence, he added, of internal unrest in Russia. Let us have no illusions about Russia's intentions, but surely a friendship treaty is just common sense. China and Russia must trade as neighbours; the Siberian pipeline is just Europe being pragmatic. The easing of tension is all that China desires. There are some critical points, such as Afghanistan and routes to the Indian Ocean. The Russians must withdraw troops from the Sino-Russian border, Cambodia and Afghanistan before any real progress can be made. Russia has armed forces four times greater than in Khruschev's time. They could invade China from Afghanistan and threaten the USA and Japan by blocking the shipping routes past Singapore. 'We should all oppose Soviet expanson,' said Mr Chang and then praised Mrs Thatcher's view of the world and her determination.

We had been talking for just over two hours and he was not finished. I was finding it difficult to follow and to keep alert. We talked about friendship. He had been in the Korean War, ran down US soldiers by criticizing their morale. He did not like President Reagan, who was just an actor, but praised Nixon and Taft, who spoke out. Nixon came to China in the interests of the American people; China mattered to them. On the other hand Reagan

154

reckoned that China needed the USA, not the other way round as Nixon had said. Reagan was making a big mistake. Then he set about flattering the British, how our common aim was to defend world peace. It was in our interest. We had had too many wars, now we deserved peace. We were both on the side of justice, just like Britain was in 1940. I must keep an open mind and stick to my noble ideals. He had had dealings with the Russian KGB since 1950; they had a huge embassy in Beijing, an invasion of agents had occurred. Our friendship would continue, our common cause was to frustrate the Soviet Union. Our informal relationship must never be detrimental to the interests of China or the United Kingdom. He was worried about the KGB in England and talked about Blunt, saying there would be more revelations.

He then talked about intelligence in general, saying that the British were extremely good at it, whereas the KGB got a man by his pigtails and shook him. Chinese intelligence started in Shanghai in 1920 and the methods used were influenced by Chairman Mao, whatever that meant. The traditional Chinese way was to make friends. The CIA and KGB methods were not for them. They were too brutal and direct. They used coercion, threats, bribes and girls. This was apparently not how the Chinese did things. The Russians used girls to blackmail people. They photographed the President of Indonesia being fondled by two naked girls and when he did not agree to co-operate they showed him the pictures. To their astonishment he was not embarrassed, said his wife would never believe him and could he please be given copies. I became alarmed when it seemed that he expected me to sign up with them. 'We were never to try and impose our will on each other. You must watch out because the KGB are everywhere, even in your country.'

He then asked, 'Have you any questions?'

I replied, 'We have been talking for three hours and I do not even know who you are! I would much appreciate it if you could tell me who you are and write your name in my pocket book.' There was much laughter. We then walked the length of the building to have an excellent dinner, tiny crabs in their shells, jellyfish, lots of *matoi* to drink and, most unusual in Chinese cooking, a sort of birthday gateau. There were many toasts and we parted in high spirits. I had been there from three-thirty until nearly nine o'clock and was exhausted.

The next day we flew to Shanghai. An unfriendly, sinister man, whom I had noticed on arrival, now took care of our tickets and baggage. A very efficient officer or agent met us in Shanghai. He spoke the local dialect and Li explained that a Beijing accent would not have had the same effect. He was about forty-five years old; he spoke no English and had a daughter. We climbed into another 'Red Flag' car and drove into Shanghai, which is completely different from Beijing. It bubbles with life, the streets are narrower and there are some magnificent old European residences and Chinese houses with balconies. There are so many people that they do not all take the same rest day, otherwise places like the Bund where people promenade would be overcrowded.

The History Museum contained a remarkable collection of bronze and porcelain and there were also two lifesize soldiers and a horse from the excavations at Xian. We had dinner at the old French club, a faded empty building and a mild culinary disaster, but they had tried hard. 'Buster' had apparently recommended the French cuisine and Li joked about how awful it had been for the next two days.

At dinner Li began his questions again. Did the British Embassy know I was in Shanghai? Who in London knew I was here? I began to hear alarm bells. If nobody knew where I was I could quite easily disappear.

'How was I going to communicate with him,' he asked, 'especially anything classified?'

I replied, 'Do not expect me to send you confidential material.'

Next day we drove to Suhzou, a town likened to Venice in that it had hundreds of bridges and many canals. Li sat in front and I sat behind, holding those infernal brown curtains back so that I could see. It was 7.30 am; it was drizzling, it was a flat, watery countryside and hundreds of people were already working in the fields. They all seemed to have a hoe raised above their shoulder, chopping at the heavy black soil. Others, heads bent down, with sickle in hand were cutting rice. It poured with rain all day, yet on our return at 4 pm they were still hard at it. The rice lay where it had been cut or in brown heaps on the edge of fields or even beside the road. Occasionally there was a water buffalo ploughing and, very rarely, a motorized tractor-cum-plough with belt transmission to the front wheels. Hundreds of bicycles filled the road, carrying all sorts of boxes and cages with chickens or vegetables; one man carried four piglets, two slung each side. Every spare bit of verge beside the road or canal was a cultivated allotment stuffed with healthy vegetables. The waterways were used to move produce direct to the towns. The boats carried piles of straw, sugar beet or boxes of cabbages. Some boats had a square sail, others worked an oar from the stern. The lucky ones were towed by tugs.

It was the buildings that depressed me. There was a total lack of colour. The debris of building lies everywhere; it is all terribly drab and functional. Factories are worse than Soviet blocks. They are windowless concrete sheds; if there is a hole it contains no glass panes. Our Chinese driver hailed an old man to ask the way. He caught sight of me in the back and said to Li and the driver, 'I don't know,' in English and walked on. They laughed and laughed. Li tried to find the nurse who had looked after him when he had heart trouble, but it was her day off. Lunch was in a private upper room in a hotel crowded with tourists, and then we visited a few temples in the rain. A very long drive back. The 'Red Flag' car was too long and too heavy and the rear wheels were constantly getting into a skid.

On the next day we started at 4.30 am to catch the train to Hangzhou. Poor Li was a bit pushed without an ADC. He left his briefcase in the waiting room and only just retrieved it before the steam engine began to move. He then sat in silence for an hour, sometimes scribbling into his little blue note book, three pages of tiny hieroglyphics which I could not understand. We sat in dark-green padded chairs with lace-covered headrests and large pot plants on the tables. It was spotlessly clean, including the windows. Young girls in railway uniform dished out cups of tea from tall jugs with a green leaf floating on top. We passed miles of cotton fields, sugar cane and mulberry plantations like vineyards which supplied food for the silk worms.

Hangzhou is a lovely place, a little town like any in Switzerland, beside a lake with a mountain background. There are gardens, lake-side promenades and lots of tea pavilions. The girls, General Li assured me, are among the prettiest in China. They are certainly the most cheerful, their faces more oval and thinner than any I had seen. They gave the hotel a permanent hum of activity. There was an eagerness to help, so much so that when General Li ordered two special dishes to be prepared for dinner next night they appeared on the table before we had finished breakfast.

157

A flock of greenfinches were feasting on ripe figs. I set about fitting a long lens to my camera in order to get a close-up picture. A small crowd gathered, plucking at my sleeve and pointing out other curiosities such as a green frog and a huge carp. Eventually there were so many people chattering to each other that the birds flew off to a quieter spot.

Back in the hotel a notice announced that 'massage was available in the barber's shop'. I wondered whether General Li would approve, but he had a different plan and we went to visit a tea plantation. We sat in an old-fashioned council chamber while the leader of number seventeen tea brigade gave a briefing on the growing cycle of tea. Chairman Mao, who had commended him highly, had twice visited the tea brigade. There was a framed photo of that memorable occasion on the wall. He had now been allowed to branch out into the forestry and silkworm business. As we left a party of elderly ladies, walking in line abreast, came into view, sweeping the road and humming a melody.

After a steep climb of some 200 steps we reached the top of the Six Harmonies Pagoda. We gazed down on the Jiang and Quiantong Rivers. Just for a moment only, because Li now had the bit between his teeth. 'We are off to a silkworm factory, but first let's have something to eat.' A plate of freshwater crabs was brought to the table, impossible to eat with chopsticks but delicious with fingers.

During lunch Li explained that it was becoming very difficult to arrange a seat for me on a plane from Canton to Hong Kong. As this was the second time he had mentioned this I began to wonder how I was ever going to get back to England. We walked up through a valley in which numerous Buddhas had been carved into the rocks until we reached a cave from which billowed the smoke of countless joss sticks. Beyond the entrance were more statues and people deep in prayer, their heads touching the ground. Li was much amused and pointed them out to me, saying, 'Look, people praying. You had better join them if you hope to get to Hong Kong!'

We visited the botanical gardens, full of every conceivable kind of chrysanthemum, then the local museum, snakes and fish in bottles, two-headed children and a fine collection of fossils, including a complete pterodactyl. A history of the local warlords and the contents of their tombs nearly finished me, but there was still the zoo: a most depressing place with animals badly housed in small cages. The polar bears had no water, monkeys in tiny dark spaces and what water there was seemed to be stagnant and foul. We had dinner in a place recommended by the driver, who also joined us. I think he must have been more than just a driver.

After dinner Li told me that his superiors wished to pay me 'my expenses'. I protested firmly and said, 'I do not want to accept any money from you. I am most grateful, but I cannot accept.' The General then explained that what they wanted was a good friend. As an example, he cited the retired Chinese General who in 1940 had a personal friend on the German General Staff. He learnt that the Germans were going to attack the Soviet Union and tipped off Chou En-lai, who in turn warned Stalin. This was to no avail because Stalin refused to believe such a thing could happen and as a result suffered a terrible defeat.

After two brandies, Li said that I was putting him in a most embarrassing position by refusing to take the money he had been ordered to give me. He could not hand it back. Once again he went back to ex-President Nixon, who had not made any fuss about accepting money from the Chinese. 'It is an old Chinese custom. We are not buying information. We are just being friendly.' He then told me about a Cambodian Prince who took refuge in Beijing. Apparently he made a pass at a chambermaid, who objected and slapped his face. 'Not what one should do to a Prince.' She screamed and two hotel staff tied his hands behind his back. Chairman Mao was told, who immediately sent a message praising her for defending the honour of Chinese womanhood. I made a mental note not even to admire Chinese womanhood in case my refusal to accept money prompted an incident.

Next day we flew to Canton where 'Buster', all smiles, had come from Hong Kong to meet us. He showed me some of the city, but it was growing dark. The showpiece was the White Swan Hotel, still under construction, but nevertheless I was given a splendid suite of rooms. 'Buster' invited me to join him for dinner in a private room where he had arranged an amazing banquet. It was a most enjoyable occasion. The manager had a daughter working in Chelsea. I wondered in which Chinese restaurant and I promised to visit the place on my safe return to London. Then, as if by magic, 'Buster' produced a ticket for my flight to Hong Kong next morning. General Li, I noticed, was most uneasy and preoccupied. Meanwhile 'Buster' had ideas of starting a business importing giant prawns direct into the King's Road, Chelsea.

I went to bed mightily relieved that my problems were nearly over. Then the door flew open and Li walked straight in without an interpreter and locked the door. He was holding a fat white envelope which he placed firmly on the bedside table. Drawing on all his limited reserves of the English language, he said, 'It will be a catastrophe for me, a disaster, if you do not accept. You must understand that I cannot give it back.'

He was visibly terribly distressed. I had never seen him lose his composure before.

'All right,' I said with great reluctance. 'I will take it to Hong Kong and leave it in a bank. I shall arrange for it to be given to the welfare of the families of Chinese seamen who were injured serving on ships of the Royal Navy in the Falklands War. I will also leave it to the needy families of Chinese soldiers serving in the Royal Hong Kong Regiment who took part in the interception of illegal immigrants. Nobody will ever know where the money came from.'

The look on his face said everything. He was a changed man. 'And please,' he added, 'on no account let "Buster" know what we have agreed.'

We parted in an affectionate mood and I thanked him for a wonderful visit to China, which I would never forget. Thus ended ten days in which I had spent the greater part of each day in his company. We had had lots of laughs together, but the visit must have put as great a strain on him as on myself.

On my return to London the gentlemen who had encouraged me to travel to China lost no time in coming to see me. They said that they were very pleased and keenly interested in what I had to tell them. But there was a very senior officer in the Ministry of Defence who was not at all pleased. He refused to believe that anyone in the Department of Defence could have been involved or that I had informed my friend in the Embassy in advance of my visit. However, his staff supported me and agreed to my draft thankyou letter, which I had been forbidden to write. So this storm over a cup of China tea was allowed to die down.

Chapter 19

BEYOND BEAR ISLAND
(See map on p. 134)

I made the first of four trips to the Svalbard Archipelago (Spitz-bergen) in 1981 at the suggestion of Commander Angus Erskine, Royal Navy, retired. He had spent two years living in East Green-land and must surely be one of the few British serving officers to have knowledge of handling a team of huskies. On one memorable occasion, while crossing a very difficult stretch for the dogs, he struggled to drag the sledge himself. When he chanced to look back over his shoulder he discovered that the dogs had all hopped onto the sledge and were enjoying the ride!

The best introduction to Svalbard is to visit the excellent Arctic museum in Tromsö in north Norway. In Longyearbyen there is another small museum with a most evocative display. Indeed, the museum is about the only place to visit in the town, which is named after a very rich American, John Longyear, who first came as a tourist in 1901. A few years later he founded the Arctic Coal Company. The settlement prospered and became Longyear City (now Longyear-byen). The coalmines were taken over by the Norwegian Govern-ment and were worked until after the Second World War, when pro-duction ceased to be profitable.

In a corner of this small museum there is a reconstruction of a trapper's log cabin. There are no local building materials, stones are scarce and difficult to lift out of the frozen soil. There are no trees and nothing grows taller than a few centimetres. However, there is plenty of timber washed up on the shores of Arctic islands, which may have been drifting for fifty years or longer. These logs, whitened by sun and salt, probably drifted down to the Arctic Ocean from the forests of Siberia on immense Russian rivers such as the Yenisei and the Lena. There is a display of old photographs, showing a bearded

161

Norwegian fur trapper who is remembered because he spent seventeen solitary winters in the High Arctic, winters when it stays dark all day long, with no communications to the outside world whatsoever.

Apparently, he met his end fighting a polar bear. There, leaning against the door of the cabin, was his rusty long-barrelled gun with the breech open. It was evident that one bullet had been fired and that the cartridge case split, because it was still there. He must then have realized that he was not going to be able to push another round into the breech and fire another shot. Grabbing his rifle by the barrel and swinging his useless weapon like a club, possibly getting one blow in before the wooden butt snapped and the bear killed and ate him. Bears are now protected and must never be shot unless a life is seriously threatened.

Safe from bears, we were travelling on a small motor vessel, registered in Amsterdam. We edged our way up the western side of Svalbard. The ship had a strengthened hull and we hoped that the ice had receded far enough northwards to enable us to reach North East Land. There were two rifles on board, one held by an Amsterdam policeman and the other by Angus, to protect us from surprise attack by polar bears.

Willem Barents, a Dutchman, discovered Bear Island in 1596, and Spitzbergen a week later. It was fitting, perhaps, that our little ship had come from Amsterdam and that the ten passengers included six Dutch and four British. I am not sure how many Dutch crew there were but we were all acutely conscious of a stocky, vibrant, red-headed crew-member called Wilhelmina, who handled the levers controlling the capstan like a magician about to reveal a new trick.

The discovery of Svalbard prompted Britain and Holland to believe that a shorter northern sea route to the treasures of China and India might yet be found. They had, however, been discouraged by powerful Spanish and Portuguese fleets which already dominated the warmer southern routes.

Early reports indicated that there were lots of whales and walrus to be found in the seas around Spitzbergen. There was already a demand for blubber, oil, tusks and leather from merchants in Europe. This prompted an Englishman called Stephen Bennet to land on Bear Island in 1604 where he found that there were hundreds of walrus resting on the foreshore. The English hunters were unskilled and turned out to be quite hopeless. In the following years, however, greed took a hand in the business. A great number of walrus were killed, culminating in the grisly total of over 600 animals killed on one day in 1606. Not surprisingly, that left scarcely any animals alive on Bear Island. Hundreds of ships and thousands of men, from many nations, were involved in this uncontrolled plunder of the Arctic Ocean. The processing of the whales by removing the blubber off the carcasses took place on shore bases such as the one on Amsterdam Island. I was still able to make out the outline of the old buildings on the seashore and the remains of the furnaces. As we approached the island I noted that there was a slight difference of opinion about something on the bridge. I hoped it was not a row about navigation because there is another much larger Amsterdam Island in the southern Indian Ocean, almost in Antarctica. This was presumably also discovered by a Dutchman, but, curiously, that island belongs to France. In 1981 I was offered a place on a ship replenishing the bases on Amsterdam, Kerguelen, Crozet and St Paul Islands. Stupidly I turned it down because I learnt that the ship had been designed for military landings in shallow waters. I feared that in the storms of the Southern Oceans the ship would roll and I would be terribly ill. I have regretted this decision ever since.

A short distance away lies Danskøya, an island, presumably named by a Dane from where an ill-fated expedition to the North Pole took off in 1897. The whole idea of getting to the Pole captured the headlines, and various attempts were made, the craziest of all perhaps was to fly there and back by hot-air balloon. A Swedish inventor and aeronaut called Salomon Andrée selected Danskøya as a good place on which to inflate a balloon because it was the shortest distance to the Pole. The balloon had been stitched together in Paris and transported by ship to Spitzbergen. He gathered a number of wealthy people to finance his attempt, including the dynamite manufacturer Alfred Nobel. He also recruited a physicist and amateur photographer, Nils Strindberg, and a meteorologist, Dr Nils Ekholm. They had the same first name.

The first thing Andrée had to do on Danskøya island was to construct a sixty-foot-high balloon hangar to protect the balloon from wind damage when it was inflated. Traces of this timber construction can still be seen. Hydrogen gas had to be manufactured on the island and this presented a huge logistic problem. The chemistry was relatively simple: pour sulphuric acid on to metal filings in a huge boiler. Trap the resultant gas under a special hood and feed it into the mouth of the balloon. Huge earthenware jars made by Doulton in London were used to carry the acid. A great many wooden barrels, packed with belt-buckles, chains, horseshoes, scrap iron and surplus metal fittings, had to be transshipped ashore and then dragged up to the gas-making contraption by two miserable ponies. The balloon was going to take many more hours to inflate than they expected. They were already far behind their schedule and there were still so many gas leaks in the balloon that the crew refused to fly until the holes were repaired. The winds from the south never blew and the weather steadily got worse, so they rolled it all up and went back to Paris, together with the fleet of tourist ships that had assembled to see the take-off. Four carrier pigeons were released, announcing the postponement of the expedition.

In 1897 Andrée returned with a new crew and a repaired balloon. More barrels of scrap metal and jars of sulphuric acid were unloaded. The remains of these can still be seen 100 years later, although each time I visited the site more of the metal had rusted away into a yellow powder. Andrée held a lunch party before take-off. There was a white tablecloth and a meal cooked by the chef from the support ship. Andrée was much concerned with the cooking facilities and had devised an oven which was to hang 26 feet below the balloon basket, lit by a rope from the basket and watched over by mirrors.

Contemporary reports say that Andrée was unhappy about the take-off and left the decision to his crew, saying, 'My comrades insist on starting, and as I have no valid reasons against it, I shall agree to it; although with some reluctance.'

He named the balloon *Eagle* and climbed aboard. After three cheers for 'good old Sweden' the balloon was cut free. Things began to go wrong almost immediately. The balloon cleared the hangar and drifted out over the sea, but then dipped suddenly into the water. The crew threw out a huge amount of vital ballast and the balloon began to climb once more. One of the ground crew then noticed that the heavy drag ropes which were part of the balloon's rudimentary steering system were still on the ground. Andrée had fitted quick-release bolts on each rope in case it caught on an iceberg or rock. As it spiralled upwards out of the hangar some of the ropes caught, the safety bolts opened and the balloon soared up, the gas expanded, safety valves opened and the balloon lost half its lifting power in the first moments after launch. A few hours later they encountered thick fog and unanticipated heavy moisture on the outer skin which almost brought the balloon down. They released homing pigeons and dropped message buoys. The balloon basket was now being dragged, lifted and then bounced on the ice; it had become an awful journey. The final psychological blow came when a large unknown black bird circled the balloon and they passed over a patch of blood-stained ice, the remains of a polar bear's dinner. Then, as the ice-encrusted fabric got heavier and heavier, they jettisoned everything, but to no avail. Eventually, on 14 July, 1897, they sank down onto the ice and jumped out. Of the pigeons released, only one was ever recovered, having been shot by a man out seal-hunting. The message on its leg gave their position 'Lat 82.2, Long 15 E good speed. All well. Andrée.'

And that was that. Nothing more was ever heard from Andrée. Just as happened after the disappearance of Lord Lucan in London sixty or so years later, Andrée was seen all over the Arctic, in Siberia, in Greenland, in San Francisco, in visions, mining gold at Klondike in the Yukon, eaten by cannibals. He was officially declared dead in 1902. Wax models of Andrée and his crew were exhibited at Madame Tussaud's Wax Museum in London, until an army of hungry mice ate the models. Thirty-three years later a Swedish scientific expedition on its way to Franz Josef Land landed on remote and rarely visited White Island. This island is normally covered in ice, but this summer it had been warm enough to thaw two narrow strips of open beach at either end. The scattered remains of Andrée's camp were visible, with a kerosene stove, a supply of fuel, mono-grammed napkins, metal crockery, a few books, a sledge still laden with supplies and a boat still lashed to it. There was the skeleton of a polar bear and a headless human torso, as well as a pair of human legs indicating that the bears had had their revenge. One body lay buried under a pile of stones, indicating he had died first. In the clothing the scientists found Andrée's diaries, letters and Strind-berg's almanac. Quite astonishingly, sealed in a metal canister, they found about fifty negatives of which twenty were still in good enough condition to be processed and can be seen in the Arctic museum at Tromsö.

Together with the diaries, they described what had happened. They were trying to walk to Cape Flora on Franz Josef Land 200

165

miles away. But the ice, they eventually realized, was drifting in the opposite direction. They died in spite of having food, fuel and a tent. At one time they were eating a kilogram of polar bear meat a day. Andrée's diary becomes like a cook book: 'Raw bear with salt tastes like oysters; we hardly wanted to fry it'. The meat, however, was so tough that it bent the metal cutlery. The best bits, he wrote, were tongue, kidney and brains. Nevertheless they all became ill and died.

Years later scientists compared the symptoms as recorded in the diary to those suffered by an Inuit tribe in Greenland in 1947. There was an outbreak of trichinosis, a horrible disease caused by tiny worms found in the raw flesh of certain wild animals which eat away at the muscles from within. This might have been the cause of their death. Freezing to death was possible, because their clothing was thin and unsuitable, but there was still plenty of layers they could have worn, and a spare sleeping bag lay alongside their bodies. Andrée's diary records how they gradually got weaker. His body was taken back to Stockholm, where he was given a State Funeral and the Air Force flew in formation over the Royal Yacht carrying his coffin. He has become Sweden's most famous explorer.

The most northern 'city' in the world, Ny-Alesund, lies about 50 kilometres south of Danskoya Island beside Kongsfjord. In 1917 coal mining began, initially with the task of refuelling the sealers. A small-gauge railway line was laid from the mines to the quayside. A tank engine with a tall smokestack, bright red buffers and four wagons can still be seen beside the water. The Arctic tern lays its eggs on the ground. They constantly take off to divebomb intruders, like myself, and anything they consider might be a threat to their eggs. People are encouraged, for safety's sake, to walk holding a stick over their heads in the same way that Second World War barrage balloons were used to keep enemy dive bombers away. Their frantic pecking can be quite disturbing! Wandering among the dwellings there are wild reindeer, the old ones seem to be quite possessive about their own territory.

Opposite Ny-Alesund is Blomstrandhalvoya where the remains of another British enterprise that failed can still be seen. In 1904 an English clergyman called F. G. Gardner, on holiday, found traces of gold. On his return to England he told a good friend, Ernest Mansfield, an industrialist, about his find. The following year Mansfield visited Spitzbergen and began to search for precious metals. He found hardly any precious metal but discovered substantial deposits of marble. He built a camp on a narrow peninsula which he called 'Camp Mansfield'. This is still visible, carved in wood above the door of a hut built on a bank above the sea shore. By 1911 he employed forty Scottish workmen, who built a quay and installed some huge pieces of machinery. Two years later it was decided that the marble was poor quality and cracked easily and that the mineral deposits were worthless too. The redoubtable Wilhelmina climbed all over the rusty steam-driven machinery with her Dutch friends and then ran down to the beach to catch a rubber dingy returning to the ship.

International interest in flying to the North Pole continued long after Andrée's disappearance in 1897. Like the relics on Dansk Island, there is a squat iron mooring mast for airships which can still be seen at Ny-Alesund. Various attempts to overfly the Arctic Ocean in Dornier seaplanes and a Junkers monoplane had ended in disaster. Roald Amundsen, a Norwegian explorer, who had already sailed round the Arctic Ocean and through the North-East Passage from Norway to the Bering Straits, was convinced that somewhere between the Pole and North America there was unmapped land, which, when he found it, he would call it Amundsen Land. He got the backing of an enthusiastic American, Lincoln Ellsworth, who agreed that an airship was probably a safer way to make the attempt. The airship, which had been named *Norge*, became the focus of international attention and rivalry. It had been handed over to the Norwegians by the Italian dictator, Mussolini, who expected Colonel Umberto Nobile to pilot the airship. The crew of sixteen included six Italians, eight Norwegians, Ellsworth and Amundsen, for whom, according to one account, two red velvet chairs had been provided. I must not forget the seventeenth member of the expedition, Titina, Nobile's dog, which had been provided with a custom-made jacket.

On 11 May, 1926, at Ny-Alesund they eased *Norge* out of her hangar and took off. Amundsen could not stand the posturing Italian. When they flew over the North Pole they released small Norwegian and American flags. Nobile, however, produced a huge Italian flag which he had difficulty in getting out of the cabin window. It got stuck to the back of the airship and threatened to get tangled with the propeller. After an epic journey they eventually came down in Alaska near a small settlement called Teller, which is on the coast of Norton Sound, to the north of Nome. The crew, having been ordered to bring the minimum baggage, were astonished that Nobile was able to put on his dress uniform. Sadly the *Norge* was destroyed by the wind at its moorings a few hours later. Amundsen, in his memoirs written in 1927, was very bitter: 'I was delighted to share the national honours with my American friend. I did not intend, however, to share them with the Italians. We owed them nothing but the opportunity to buy and pay for a second-hand military dirigible.'

Nobile returned to Spitzbergen after making a triumphant tour of predominatly Italian cities in the USA. He then made a number of exploratory flights over Arctic islands in another airship. Amundsen was understandably not only very bitter at the adulation Nobile received, but also because he had made the role of explorer become one of just sitting on a velvet chair and looking out of a misty window. Nobile was received by the Pope who gave him a large wooden cross to drop on to the Pole the next time he flew over it.

The next flight, in spring, 1928, encountered many difficulties and eventually on the return flight to Ny-Alesund it crashed into the frozen sea. The cabin and front of the airship broke off, being that much lighter, but the rear section took off again, taking six Italian crewmen with it. They were never seen again. Finland, Norway, Sweden and France launched a huge international rescue operation. Amundsen, in spite of his feelings towards Nobile, volunteered to accompany a Dornier seaplane, lent by the French, in the search. It was some days before Nobile's SOS call was picked up by a young Russian farmer 1,400 miles away. It was not until several days later that the rescue could be completed. During the search Amundsen's aircraft went missing and a Swedish plane overturned landing near the wreck. This had been located by a Russian ice-breaker, the *Krassin*, which was running out of fuel and had damaged a propeller when it found them. Nobile and his dog were picked up before his crew. He was reviled and branded a coward; the crash was blamed on him as was the fact that a man was left to die on the ice by his colleagues. Such was the despair in Norway at Amundsen's disappearance that when Nobile's support ship, *Citta di Milano*, arrived in Narvik from Spitzbergen a special walkway had been constructed from the ship to his train so that he would not step on Norwegian soil. He was treated very shabbily by his country, but the Swedes awarded him the Andrée medal and the Russians put him in charge of their airship building. He moved to the USA in 1936 where he lived in exile until he returned to Italy in 1946. Eventually his reputation was restored and he died aged ninety-one. The airship mooring mast and a monument to Roald Amundsen at Ny-Alesund are reminders of the epic achievements of both men. Together they had been the first to fly over the North Pole.

Ny-Alesund is the most northerly permanently inhabited settlement in the world, founded in 1916. Not surprisingly there is a special postmark which is sold at the only shop, in a corner of a barrack block. I wondered how they kept their spirits up in the long winter nights, because there is little to commend the place.

Our aim was to try to reach North East Land, if the ice had receded, and then to walk up to North Cape. We set off to the north, taking advantage of a fine weather forecast. There is a walrus reserve around Moffen Island, a circular low-lying bank of gravel with a lagoon inside. We waited a few hours, but for some reason the dozens of seals and walrus who bask on the bank went elsewhere. Further north, on Murchison Fjord, are the remains of an Oxford University expedition to North East Land made in the early 1930s. An old kitchen grate is wedged between two rocks and the remains of a wooden hut are visible. One side has been blown down and I doubt whether it will last many more years. Stout wooden boxes which contained their provisions lie broken, with their address burnt onto the lids. It was fascinating to read the old newspapers which had been used as insulation in the wall of the hut. We put them back carefully. A large polar bear could be seen approaching, so we halted near a small iceberg and waited. Standing on two feet on an ice floe, the bear was able to reach the deck. Wilhelmina appeared from the galley with a loaf of bread on a rope which she dangled over the beast's nose. By the time she had been told to pack it in, he, for it was a male, had snatched it from her and if she had not let go would probably have got her as well.

Eventually we crossed Lat 80. 30 and anchored in a little bay below North Cape. I set out with Angus to walk to the top of the cliff and look towards the Pole beyond the tiny Sjuoyane Islands 5 miles away. When we returned to the beach a huge bonfire had been lit, using logs as big as telegraph poles. Floating a few feet away was a small iceberg; undaunted, many of the crew, including Wilhelmina, took off what they could and jumped into the icy water. Blue with cold, they huddled half-naked round a fire and sang until the Amsterdam policeman suggested that, in spite of their Dutch courage, they should return to the ship before freezing.

About 20 kilometres east of North Cape there is a region full of small fjords and creeks in which the Germans established a secret weather station in 1944. Four men and their equipment had been taken there by submarine, which then sailed away and was lost at sea. The only people left who knew of the station's existence and who remained in radio contact were at Naval Headquarters in Berlin, which capitulated to the Russians on 1 May, 1945. By the late summer of that year they began to realize that nobody knew of their existence and that they had better prepare for the winter. They were fortunate to be seen by a Norwegian sealing boat making a rare trip round North East Land, a situation similar to that of the German scientists who were abandoned in the South Atlantic on Bouvet Island in 1939 when the war began. They were lucky to be found in 1943 by a Royal Navy destroyer crewed by Norwegian sailors.

The quartermaster on our ship now chose to reveal that in the bilge he had a store of wine bottles which, as we were sailing back to Longyearbyen, he offered for sale at a very special price. We had a memorable party in the course of which I asked Wilhelmina if she was happy to be going home to Holland.

'I am staying,' she replied. 'I am going to spend the winter with a trapper in his hut, just to test myself through six months of darkness.'

'Do you know the man?' I asked. 'Does he speak any language you know?'

'No,' she said, 'but he was pointed out to me in a bar and seemed a nice chap. Do not worry,' she added with a charming smile, 'I will not get pregnant.'

I admired her pragmatic approach, but have always wondered how it worked out.

Chapter 20

SPITZBERGEN AT WAR
(See map on p. 134)

It was my third visit and I felt sure that something must by now have changed in Barentsberg, a most depressing Russian settlement on Green Fjord in the Norwegian Archipelago of Svalbard. Sure enough, at the top of the 200 or so slippery wooden steps from the quayside the statue of Lenin, which had cast a baleful spell over the miserable settlers for the past sixty or so years, had at last been removed. So too had the giant notice board covered with photos of the best coal miner of the month, the best vegetable gardener, the most vigilant block manageress and countless minor Party officials. Communism had failed. The news had only just begun to dawn on the inhabitants of Barentsberg and the other Russian coal-mining village, Pyramiden.

The inhabitants set up their stalls on tables half-way up the steps and were at last allowed to become capitalists. They offered flags, fur hats, sweaters, military uniforms, including that of an Air Force General, lumps of coal containing exquisite fossils of ancient tropical vegetation, clogs, Party badges, postcards and various bottles containing dubious alcoholic spirits. The only currency they all wanted was United States dollar bills. Why on earth do we worry about the Euro when all corners of the world seem happy to accept the American dollar?

The presence of coal seams so near to the surface means there is never a shortage of hot water to heat the hideous barrack blocks, the greenhouses and the cowsheds. Ira was immensely proud of her achievements and grew fresh vegatables in small quantities. She insisted that visitors bought a polar bear tiepin before being taken on a conducted tour of her hothouse. Further down the muddy track there was a herd of about thirty cows and numerous swine, which

171

were never going to see, let alone chew, a blade of grass. It was amazing to see sweet peas in flower, when outside the ground was covered in snow except where the permafrost had been broken by vehicles to reveal an inch or so of mud. In the accommodation area there was a gymnasium, a large heated swimming pool and a library with a few shelves of well-thumbed paperback Russian novels. The small museum had a natural history display in which some of the creatures were hardly recognizable after the taxidermist had finished with them. The twentieth-century history of Barentsberg was well illustrated, but the captions were only what the curator, a grey-haired Party official, felt we should know. It was only on this, my third visit, that, 'in view of the changing political situation', she accepted my corrections with good grace. It concerned the events of the Second World War, when Svalbard was of vital strategic importance to both sides.

In 1773 a British naval party, which included Midshipman Horatio Nelson and a few scientists, landed for a short stay. It is unlikely that they realized what mineral resources existed, let alone what the strategic value of weather forecasts from the top of the world would be 150 years later. A network of meteorological stations had been established long before war began in 1939. These sent out regular weather forecasts. One was located at Kap Linné on Spitzbergen, but there were other Meteorological Stations on Bear Island, Jan Mayen Island and Greenland.

The Allies soon realized the value of Spitzbergen, with its great reserves of coal and its strategic position from whence German submarines could threaten ships carrying vital supplies from Britain to the hard-pressed Russians in Murmansk. The chance to set up their own weather stations would be an invaluable prize for the Germans. Convinced that they must have already occupied Spitzbergen, the British hurriedly assembled an invasion force to retake the island. However, a reconnaissance, probably by a submarine, showed that the Germans had not yet landed. In view of the fact that winter was expected soon, the British decided to forestall the enemy by sailing immediately. This small force was ordered to destroy the existing facilities and to evacuate the Norwegian and Russian inhabitants.

A great deal of diplomacy was going to be needed. An English-speaking official from the Russian Embassy and a Russian-speaking officer from the War Office took the night train to Scotland to join the expedition. The Russian carried a letter signed by their Ambassador, Mr Maisky, with specific instructions to the Russian Commissar in Barentsberg, known as the 'Consul'.

The force was to be transported on the liner *Empress of Canada* with an escort of five warships including the cruiser *Nigeria*, which carried the overall commander of the expedition, Admiral Sir Philip Vian. The soldiers were all Canadian except for a platoon of Norwegians and a detachment from the Royal Army Service Corps. They were commanded by Brigadier Potts, a Canadian. The force set sail in haste and in great secrecy. It was the end of August, 1941, and a period of continuous daylight. The ships refuelled off Bear Island where there was the constant risk of the ships being spotted by German aircraft and their position being passed to U-boats or to German battleships hiding in the Norwegian fjords. The plan, which assumed that there were no German troops on Spitzbergen, was to pick up the 2,000 or so Russians in Barentsberg and take them to Archangel. While this was going on Brigadier Potts' task was to destroy anything that might help the Germans, but leaving the mineshafts intact should it ever be possible to reopen them. The Norwegian miners, together with the Canadian soldiers, were to embark on the *Empress of Canada* when she returned from Archangel and be taken to Britain.

The small fleet anchored in the fjord opposite Barentsberg. To a casual historian it must have appeared that the British had not learnt much since the disastrous amphibious landing at Gallipoli in the First World War. The assault troops, a platoon of Canadian riflemen, set out for the shore in a ship's lifeboat. A second lifeboat carried the Brigadier, his headquarters staff and the two liaison officers from London. They were met, according to reports at the time, by a suspicious crowd of Russians, completely under the control of the political Commissar who styled himself the 'Consul'. He exerted his authority through a network of loudspeakers and a number of black-leather-jacketed officials. He refused to acknowledge the contents of Mr Maisky's letter brought from London, because the letter only 'invited him to comply with British instructions'. Anyway, it was quite impossible, he insisted, for the Russians to leave for at least three days and until they had had further confirmation from Moscow. It was strongly put to him that, because of the threat posed by U-boats, they must sail that very evening.

The Russians had not come willingly to Barentsberg to work in the mines and they were only too happy to leave. There had been very few married quarters and men and women lived in single-sex dormitories. There was very little sanitation. Sewage and rubbish were piled in heaps outside the settlement where a colony of Glaucous gulls kept the smell under control. Indeed, it was an offence to harm these noisy birds which, together with the intense cold, prevented an outbreak of disease. To this day they still nest under the eaves of the green administration building which stands at the top of the steps from the quayside.

There was a Russian mining company shop, 'Trust Arktigul', which sold a limited selection of goods. It was not allowed to sell spirits, in fact only the 'Consul' was allowed to stock any drink, a privilege which no doubt gave him considerable patronage over the rest. The one memory many Canadians retained was the extraordinary sickly-sweet odour which hung over the place. The Russians had managed to get round the restriction on alcohol by buying vast quantities of cheap *eau de cologne*. They drank so much of this that the smell exuded through the pores of their skin.

By midday about 1,500 miners with their baggage were on the quay waiting to be ferried by a destroyer out to the *Empress of Canada* which lay at anchor in the middle of the fjord. Many had put on their best clothes, carried their winter coats and were in high spirits. Nevertheless, there were still about 300 of the Consul's close supporters who showed no intention of wishing to leave until he gave the order and that seemed unlikely.

Once again the Russian-speaking English officer climbed up the steps to the administration building where he found the Consul to be firm and friendly, and politely offered him a glass of wine. They had a few more glasses before the Englishman excused himself and managed to get a large group of Russians moving past the Consul's piquet at the top of the steps. The official from the Russian Embassy in London who had carried the Maisky letter now decided to change sides so to speak and support the Consul. He was tricked back on board the destroyer and locked in a cabin.

The loudspeakers, which had been going nonstop with martial music and instructions to stay put, were now sabotaged by Canadian signallers. The Consul, who was in an expansive mood, now opened a bottle of Georgian champagne and another bottle of Ukrainian vodka. The end was fast approaching. The Consul was persuaded to sign a paper which said he was leaving Barentsberg of his own free will. This was to the fury of the vice-consul. There was just time for one more toast to Marshal Stalin and Mr Churchill before he slid gently beneath the table. The British took a few quick photographs of the recumbent Consul and then lifted him on to a stretcher. It must have been a difficult task for the sailors taking him down the wooden steps rather like a mountain rescue team. In order to save face, the stretcher was accompanied down the steps by a uniformed nursing sister who held his hand. The Consul's piquet suddenly vanished and minutes later appeared with their bags already packed at the top of the steps. Their departure was watched by Canadian troops as they jostled to get on board the waiting destroyer. It was a photograph of this event that I drew to the attention of the stern lady museum curator, who had once explained to me how the Russian Army and Navy had carried out the timely evacuation in 1941 right under the eyes of the Germans.

'Look at the tin helmets.'

I pointed out to her the webbing and small packs, the ground sheets, the ancient water bottles and the Light Machine Gun (a Bren gun) on its bipod in the foreground.

'How can you possibly mistake those Canadian soldiers for the superbly equipped Russian Army?'

She had to agree. I gave her a pen with which she amended the captions then and there.

Meanwhile, the early arrivals on the liner had had time to run wild and explore the ship. They chose whatever cabin suited them best. Anybody who had encountered the Russians in the Second World War might recall their total ignorance of what to do with western plumbing. The mess and the smell were indescribable after a few hours on board. The late arrivals, however, were part of the Consul's elite hierarchy and insisted that they should have the best cabins. It took the ship's crew a further hour to reallocate the cabins. It was not possible to put all the women into cabins, so the rest of the women were put in a lounge which was supposed to be secure. Of course it was not and an orgy of open love-making began, which only ceased for a few moments to allow meals to be served.

The ship sailed on time, leaving soldiers to destroy the stocks of oil and machinery before it returned to bring them back to Britain. So far they had not been spotted because the local meteorological station continued to send false reports of low clouds which made aerial reconnaissance impossible. There were a few Norwegians in Longyearbyen who just did not want to leave the quiet life and the good pay they earned working in an Arctic coalfield. They imagined that their action would deny coal supplies to their countrymen in Northern Norway. This stalemate continued until three ships arrived to collect coal specifically for German occupation forces in Norway. The Norwegian doubters needed little further persuasion to join the Allies.

The arrival and departure of the ships was reported to German Headquarters in Northern Norway as was the routine. But once clear of Svalbard they sailed for Scotland with prize crews. Meanwhile, the work of destroying anything that might be of value to the Germans continued. The clouds of black smoke which filled the air were surely going to be seen by reconnaissance aircraft, had they still not been heeding the false weather reports. In Barentsberg the fires spread and a wooden building caught fire. This continued to spread and every single sailor and soldier was trying to damp down the flames. After a few hours they succeeded, but next day the wind fanned the embers and in the end half Barentsberg was burnt to the ground.

The *Empress of Canada* hit the most awful weather and the mess and confusion on board only got worse. The misuse of washbasins added to the stench of seasick passengers. It might, however, have kept enemy warships in port. One report tells of the consternation when small items such as socks, which had been put into a water closet to rinse, disappeared when flushed, never to be seen again. There was too the inescapable smell of all that cheap *eau de cologne* which they had been unable to leave behind.

It took four days to reach the mouth of the Dvina on which the city of Archangel is situated. Although the British and Canadians were wartime allies of the Soviet Union, none of them were allowed to step ashore. The Russian passengers were disembarked, including a pregnant lady who gave birth as her feet touched dry land. She had held back the birth for the whole journey because she was terrified for the safety of the child if it was not born on Russian soil.

While they were unloading in the pouring rain a barge came along-side containing men in the most terrible state. Their clothes were in tatters and they did not seem to have eaten a proper meal for weeks. They were British and French prisoners of war who had been captured in 1940. They had escaped from German prisons and headed for Poland and the Baltic States in the hope that their allies, the Russians, would repatriate them. They were moved from prison to prison, including the dreaded Ljubianka in Moscow. They were kept in appalling conditions and not even the Red Cross had access to them. Finally they were moved to a camp near Archangel where the British Embassy heard of their plight and now they were to be set free. Once their utter disbelief that the nightmare was over sank in, their joy was overwhelming. The Canadian crew could not have been more kind or more generous. There was an added bonus in that there were a number of French Canadians on board.

The total indifference shown by the Russians to the fate of prisoners of war, whether they were allies or enemy, was not new. Stalin had imprisoned and killed millions of his own people who objected, for instance, to the collectivization of farms. In 1951 I used to meet trainloads of German prisoners of war released from captivity in the Soviet Union. Whereas the Allies released all their prisoners within the first year of peace, these men had to wait five or six years. Some just disappeared. I remember one railway coach of older men arriving at the border between East and West Germany in 1951. They had been prisoners since the Spanish civil war in 1936. They were German merchant seamen who had been loading timber in Murmansk when they were interned by the Russians. At that time Germany supported General Franco and the Soviet Union supported the Communists. They had been totally forgotten and even when Germany and Russia became Allies in 1939 to invade Poland, they still were kept in prison.

The *Empress of Canada* set sail again for Longyearbyen from where it collected the soldiers and Norwegian miners whose work of destruction was finished. The ships then paused to pick up the Canadian garrison from Barentsberg, which was still smouldering after the drastic fire. As they sailed out into the Arctic Ocean they could hear frantic radio transmission from the Germans in Norway trying to find out what had happened to the weather stations. Admiral Vian had accomplished his task, destroyed most of the machinery and evacuated the population. However, there was still one Norwegian left behind. He was opposed to leaving and hid until the ships left. He was, however, spotted a few days later by a German reconnaissance aircraft trying to find out what had caused the radio silence from Svalbard. They returned to make a very difficult landing, and then were able to trick him into accepting a free holiday flight to his home in Norway. Only then did he realize that he had returned to a homeland occupied by the Nazis. Now that there really was nobody left on any of the islands, both the British and the Germans began to miss the invaluable weather reports and both planned to re-establish weather stations.

In 2003, when he was ninety-two years old, I had the good fortune to communicate with Sir Alexander Glen, KBE, DSC, who had been an RNVR officer at the time. He had only just returned from being assistant Naval Attaché when Yugoslavia was invaded by Germany. He was pitch-forked into joining Admiral Vian's expedition because he had visited Svalbard several times before the war. He had been the leader of the Oxford University Arctic Expedition in 1936. A few packing crate lids bearing the initials OUAE were still lying on the ground at Depotodden on North East Land in 1986 beside the remains of their hut.

Alexander Glen (who died in 2004) was one of a small group of experienced officers who tried to urge Admiral Vian to realize the importance of leaving a small force behind in order to deny the islands to the enemy. Admiral Vian, however, did not want to listen and Brigadier Potts was unimaginative and only too glad to get away. The evacuation of Norwegian and Russian miners was a humanitarian need because they would have become slave labour. However, the decision to leave Spitzbergen undefended was a crass error because the Germans immediately established secret weather stations there.

By the spring of 1942 a company of Norwegian troops had been trained in Scotland under the command of Einar Sverdrup, who had been the manager of the Norwegian Arctic Mining company in Spitzbergen. He had two distinguished American brothers, one a Rear Admiral who made his name in underwater operations and the other a Major General who built a string of landing-strips in the Pacific war. On his return to England Commander Glen was the prime mover of a Norwegian/British group encouraging an early return. The force was to embark on a small ice breaker, the *Isbjorn*, and on a sealer, the *Seles*. There were to be about sixty soldiers who all had some knowledge of Spitzbergen, together with three British liaison officers, Lieutenant Colonel Godfrey, Royal Engineers, Commander Glen, RNVR, and Lieutenant Colonel Whatman, Royal Signals.

They had to sail early in May. Ten days later RAF Catalina aircraft discovered that the Germans were already on Spitzbergen and that there was no way to warn the ships. Sverdrup, on the *Isbjorn*, had approached Barentsberg with caution and sent a ski patrol overland from Kap Linné to see if the town was occupied. It was not, but the fjord was still covered with ice. They tried to break a path through the ice with the *Isbjorn*, but it was a very slow business.

While Barentsberg was still a mile away a German aircraft was heard. It had probably spotted them before turning away. The British liaison officers warned Sverdrup that in less than six hours they would be attacked and that the ships must be unloaded immediately. Stuck in the ice, the two ships were sitting ducks. The same mistake was made as was made over the unloading of *Sir Galahad* in the Falklands War years later. A four-engine Focke Wolff Condor aircraft came in, guns blazing, followed by three more. Sverdrup ordered the men to jump onto the ice. Glen writes, 'I was on the bridge of the *Isbjorn* when the blast sucked Sverdrup and Godfrey back into the burning ship while I and Whatman were blown overboard.' The aircraft then began to machine-gun the men on the ice who had no cover whatsoever. When the Condors pulled away there was just a black hole in the ice which marked where the *Isbjorn* had sunk, which was already being covered over with ice. The little sealer *Seles* was burning, none of the stores of food, weaponry or radios had been saved. Barentsberg was still half a mile away across the ice. There were forty men still alive, fourteen had been killed, including their leader, Norwegian Colonel Einar Sverdrup and Lieutenant Colonel Godfrey.

The loss of their two leaders much affected the Norwegians, who were appalled at the blood on the snow, where your only enemy can be the weather and polar bears. Nobody knew of the disaster that had befallen the expedition; there was no way of letting the Allies know. They salvaged some medical supplies from the old hospital

179

ruins and placed the wounded in a basement. The only food found was a supply of hard-boiled sweets in a locker and some coffee. Then someone remembered that the Russians had kept pigs which were slaughtered before the Canadians left the previous summer. Eventually their frozen carcasses were found under the snow. Arctic foxes may have eaten parts, but it was a welcome if strange diet, pork, sweets and coffee. Most days the Germans flew over and fired on anyone they could see. The wounded were safe in their basement and the tiny garrison had covered themselves in white sheets and dentist jackets, which made it difficult to spot them against the snow. Their ski tracks, however, did sometimes betray their presence to German pilots, who were probably the only people to know they were there.

Sitting in a lookout shelter at Cape Heer just north of Barentsberg were Lieutenant Colonel Whatman and a soldier when on 26 May they heard an aircraft. They immediately took cover and watched it circle over the fjord leading to Barentsberg.

'It's one of ours,' shouted Whatman. 'Where is the Aldis lamp?'

This was a powerful light which they had constructed out of pieces found in a hut at Barentsberg. He aimed it at the Catalina and was delighted to get a reply. He then, using Morse code, told of the tragedy, the loss of the two ships, the casualties and the urgent need of food and weapons. The Catalina, piloted by Squadron Leader Healy, had already been airborne since the previous day, but did not waste any time. It turned round and began a fourteen-hour journey to the Shetland Islands.

Whatman's knowledge of the Morse code had proved invaluable. Two days later Healy was airborne again and the soldiers in Barentsberg were delighted when, after an incredibly long flight, the seaplane tried to find a place to land, but was frustrated by the persistent ice. Anyway, the stores were parachuted on to the ice, where many broke up, but were carefully gathered up by the starving garrison. Healy flew a third epic Arctic flight two days later and managed to find space to land in the fjord, about half a mile from the quay at Barentsberg. He and his crew then had the tedious task of transferring the supplies ashore in rubber dinghies and bringing the wounded to the Catalina. All the time there was the danger of being spotted by a German aircraft, but mercifully there was a thick cloud bank. Healy then had a difficult task taking off again and avoiding the razor-sharp pack ice. In nine days he had flown ninety-seven hours in the most appalling conditions, four extraordinary flights which changed the course of the war in the Arctic. He received the DSO and his navigator, Flight Lieutenant E. Schofield, was awarded the DFC. Sadly, in September Healy was shot down while protecting convoy PQ18 to North Russia after his machine-gun jammed. He was buried near Kildin Island, north of Murmansk.

The Norwegian garrison in Barentsberg, having now been strengthened, launched a swift attack on the Germans in Longyearbyen, only to discover that they had been airlifted out a few days before. Finally, in order to strengthen the Allied grip on Svalbard, the cruisers *Manchester* and *Sheffield*, escorted by four destroyers, landed anti-aircraft guns and equipment. Fortunately, the heavy cloud prevented the Germans knowing this had taken place.

The next unsuspecting German aircraft, piloted by Erich Ettienne, was shot down. He had been a member of several international expeditions to Svalbard in the 1930s and was well known to Alexander Glen and his friends. It is nice to know that those young German, British and Norwegian explorers who survived were able to visit each other. Their bonds of lasting friendship were forged after sharing the dangers of living in the High Arctic. The war in the Arctic was carried out by small groups of men on both sides who were sustained by aircraft or by submarines. Both the Allies and the Germans were able to establish secret weather stations which provided invaluable weather forecasts right up to the end of the war. Indeed a well-hidden German-manned weather station in North East Land lost contact with Berlin when the war ended and might in the confusion following the collapse of Germany have been completely forgotten but for a Norwegian seal hunter who found their hut in August, 1945.

The only major engagement on Svalbard took place in September, 1943, when the German battleships *Tirpitz* and *Scharnhorst*, together with ten destroyers, were ordered by Adolf Hitler to destroy the Norwegian forces at Barentsberg and Longyearbyen. This was a very one-sided affair. There were only about 100 Norwegian soldiers with three small guns against vastly superior forces. After a sharp engagement, the Norwegians inflicted heavy casualties on German soldiers standing on the decks of the destroyers. In the dust and confusion they were able to flee to higher ground and hide in the mineshafts. Their commander was captured trying to burn secret papers in his office. After six hours' bombardment, the German ships' sirens sounded, recalling the troops. The Norwegian retreat had been concealed by the smoke billowing from burning piles of coal which had been set alight by the shelling.

At Longyearbyen, which had an even smaller garrison, the gun battery was deceived by a German destroyer flying the White Ensign. It was only when the destroyers opened fire that the Norwegians replied. By then German infantry were landing behind them. Heavily outnumbered, the Norwegians retreated inland, their escape made possible by the rearguard action of a young corporal firing bursts from a Bren gun until he fell wounded. His comrades escaped from the pursuing Germans by running up the mountain and hiding in the mineshafts. Some two hours after the attack on Longyearbyen had begun, the battleship *Scharnhorst*, which had until then been refuelling a destroyer, now opened fire. She was determined not to miss this unique opportunity to fire her big guns, the only time in the Second World War. She continued to pour shells on to every possible Norwegian hideout long after blasts on the ship's siren had called the German assault troops back. Very little had escaped destruction and it does not take much imagination to look at the burnt ruins and chimney stacks as they are today to appreciate what the survivors endured before the German surface ships sailed back into hiding in Norwegian fjords. Amazingly only six Norwegians were killed.

By mid-October, 1943, the Royal Navy had returned, bringing materials and supplies to enable the small garrison to survive another winter. Barentsberg continued to be protected by a small Norwegian garrison.

Nobody seems to know what happened to the Russian Consul and his cronies. In November, 1944, the Russians, who were by now winning the war, already had troops in Kirkenes, Northern Norway. They demanded that the Treaty of 1920, which gave sovereignty of Spitzbergen to Norway and specified that it must remain neutral, should now be reconsidered. Russia had already annexed Petsamo, a port in North Finland, and parts of Eastern Finland. They had seized Latvia, Lithuania, Estonia, East Prussia and East Poland, Bukovina, Moldavia and Ruthenia in Slovakia. Two weeks before the war ended and after the second atom bomb had already been dropped on Japan, the Russians declared war on Japan and seized Sakhalin. In the Baltic they occupied the Danish island of Bornholm. They were most reluctant to leave until the local Danish Home Guard commander demanded their withdrawal. A firm stance by the Danes and Norwegians enabled the prewar status to be retained. Sadly, the rest of the Allies in 1945 acceded to Russian demands, thus proving that might is right!

Barentsberg was reoccupied by the Russians in 1946 and coal production resumed. It took them a little longer than the Norwegians to get going, but by the time I made my first visit to Barentsberg it was once again very much a Communist state, a whole world away from life in Longyearbyen. The inevitable commissar met us and insisted on our cameras being put away. We were not on that occasion encouraged to stay, so we cast off and sailed east in a sealer to Colesbukta where parts of a very long jetty of bleached timber stretched out into the bay. A mining settlement was being closed down. The desolation, the filth and despair that seemed to hang over the place reached everywhere, except the kitchen, where a dozen large ladies in white smocks and hats were delighted to see strangers. Needless to say, the inevitable commissar wearing a black leather jacket and trilby hat soon stopped the merriment. He objected to the cameras and nearly had a fit when we lined up the cooks and gave them a polaroid picture of themselves.

In a dark corner of a vast empty shed a Dutchman in our small party was negotiating with a Russian miner for the purchase of a pair of leather jackboots. He handed over the dollars and the little Russian ran off to his hut to fetch the boots. They were busy completing the deal when voices could be heard approaching. I shall never forget the look of fear on the poor fellow's face. He put the money in his pocket, flung the boots into a distant corner and fled. The commissar, for indeed it was he, saw nothing. The Dutchman was able to retrieve the boots and put them into his pack. As we returned to the boat we passed an Arctic fox, frozen stiff, beside a narrow railway which ran from the mine to the pier. The rails had once been covered by a roof which had now collapsed, but which had once enabled loading to continue in all weathers. As we cautiously crossed a gap in the broken pier a gesticulating figure in a leather jacket ran down the slope towards us.

'Oh no, not him again. Let us cast off quickly.'

Chapter 21

FRANZ JOSEF LAND
(See map on p. 134)

That two landlocked nations with no maritime tradition should have been able to form a navy was quite astonishing. The Austro-Hungarians, thanks to a tenuous link with the sea at Rijeka (Fiume), were able to make their presence felt way beyond the Adriatic Sea. Their last appearance was in the First World War, in 1916, when an Austro-Hungarian submarine surfaced in the harbour of Portoferraio on the Isle of Elba. She fired a few small shells towards the town causing widespread panic among the Italian citizens.

Among their first successes was the accidental discovery of an unknown Arctic archipelago which was then named Franz Joseph Land. It may have been sighted by Baffin in 1614, but the actual discovery and first landing were made by Julius Payer, a Lieutenant in the Austro-Hungarian Army. He left Bremen on 13 June, 1872, in a ship called the *Tegetthoff* of 220 tons, with a crew of twenty-four, which included sixteen Dalmatian seamen, a Norwegian harpooner, two Tirolean mountaineers and eight hounds. It is not clear what the hounds were expected to hunt. They certainly would not have stood much chance against a polar bear. The expedition was financed by Count Wilczek and they were able to name a large island after him. Payer's ship got caught in the ice and had to spend two winters there. Unable to sail, he set out on foot to explore neighbouring islands and named them, as was then the custom, after his ruler and benefactors. He returned to the warm Adriatic Sea with tantalizing reports of an uncharted sea and distant islands.

In 1881, a Mr Leigh Smith, on his yacht, *Eira*, explored the southern coastline and discovered many islands before returning to England. When he returned in 1882 his ship sank and he had to build an emergency hut before spending the winter on Cape Flora.

There is, among the old maps at the Royal Geographical Society, a rough plan of this hut. It was 12 metres by 4 metres, with an entry porch on one side. The bed spaces of twenty men are allotted by name in one half behind their sea chests. In the other half the Captain, Mr Bernard Leigh Smith, is next to the gun case and ammunition. Lopely, the ship's carpenter, was next to the chronometers and Dr Neal next to the medicines and wine. The first and second mates, Crowther and Fenton, were next to the pepper, curry and pickle barrels. The toughest job of all seems to have gone to the chief engineer, Robertson, who slept with three barrels of rum at his head.

Thirteen years later, in 1894, Mr Alfred Harmsworth (later Lord Northcliffe) fitted out a ship, the *Woodward*, under the leadership of Mr Frederick Jackson. His aim was to set up a permanent base to explore the unknown islands and maybe one day reach the North Pole. The ship anchored on 7 September, 1894, at 'Elmwood', named after Lord Northcliffe's country estate on the Isle of Thanet in south-east England. It was in fact Cape Flora on Northbrook Island. Two years later the Jackson–Harmsworth expedition went 70 miles north towards the Pole and named two new stretches of water 'British Channel' and 'Queen Victoria Sea'. Unknown to them, the famous Norwegian explorer, Fridtjof Nansen, had been forced to give up his attempt to drift to the North Pole. He discovered that sea currents were moving the ice, in which his ship, the *Fram*, was stuck to the south, away from the North Pole. So he left the ship with his colleague Johansen and they decided to build a winter hut near Cape Norway which, unknown to them, was only a few miles away from the spot reached by Jackson.

On 17 June, 1896, Nansen, who had been away from civilization for many months, smelled strong pollution in the air. It was Jackson's scented shaving soap and expensive perfume! Their lucky meeting saved Nansen's life and they were able to prove that there was no land between Franz Josef Land and the North Pole.

Various other men tried taking expeditions to the North Pole: Captain Robertson, a Scot; Mr Pike and Sir Savile Gossley, British; Dr Lerner and Captain Rudiger, German; Walter Wellman, an American, and the Duke of Abruzzi, an Italian, on a ship called the *Pole Star*. None ever reached the North Pole and all returned to Tromsö.

In 1913 the Tsar of Russia established a base and in 1928 the Soviet Union claimed the islands for Russia. A great silence descended and foreigners were not allowed to visit. The Russian ship *Sedov* established a meteorological station on Hooker Island, having taken a lot of timber from the old camp at Cape Flora to build it. In 1931 the Graf Zeppelin touched down on its way to the North Pole and Alaska. Ten years later the Russians on Hooker Island were abandoned to their fate for six years because of the world war. Heaven knows how they survived, let alone kept sane. During that period the Germans established a secret weather station on Alexander Isle. It was not until 1991 that the Iron Curtain lifted. I was fortunate to be a guest lecturer to the first two groups allowed to land.

There were seven hours to fill in Tromsö before sixty-one passengers arrived to board the *Klavdiya Yelanskaya*, named after a famous Russian actress who died in 1972. It was a lovely sunny spring day, the mountains still covered with snow. I was told that, in spite of a nip in the air, the first sign of sunshine after the long grey winter caused many Norwegians to lose their inhibitions. If I did not believe this I should take the lift up the mountain. Naturally I did so and, a short climb beyond the lifthead, there were a dozen or so naked girls lying on the snow in the dazzling sunshine.

The crew gave the passengers a warm welcome; only three could understand English as this was the first English-speaking group they had ever encountered. They were immaculate, the cabins spotless and the decks scrubbed clean. They politely accepted a bicycle from an earnest young man, knowing that there was not a chance of it being ridden one metre before the end of the voyage. At 8 pm we sailed. The ship slowed down at the mouth of the Tromsö Fjord for us to look at an island where thousands of sea birds nested on the steep cliffs. They were encouraged to 'show a leg' and 'flap a wing' by two blasts on the ship's siren, an incredible sight as they all took to the air at the same time.

There were many who had forgotten what it was like to be on a rolling ship scudding along into a fresh breeze. The life jackets were of circa-1939 design and we looked like Tweedledum and Tweedledee. The lifeboats had an engine and eight huge oars. Now I understood why there was a rowing machine in the gym. At 11 pm that night we dropped anchor off the south coast of Bear Island and gazed up at the fantastic high cliffs of Stoppen. It was daylight all day and, sheltered from the north winds, we watched thousands of guillemots, terns, auks and gulls swirling like bats beneath the cliffs and waterfalls. On a previous visit I recall that the wind was so strong that the waterfalls were driven vertically upwards. Looking at thirteen caves at the foot of the cliffs I wondered which had been the Pearly Gate in the novel *Bear Island* by Alistair Maclean.

Getting the passengers to time their jump into the boats to catch the rise and fall in the swell was achieved thanks to the patience and encouragement of the Russian sailors, who also put the passengers on the rocky shore. The gigantic cliffs were teeming with nests. On the shore was a solitary Glaucous gull, which could not fly, tearing away at a crab. Temporarily abandoned was a nest of Eider ducklings. Sailing up the east coast of Bear Island we passed two whalers with harpoon guns on their bows. Had the Norwegians begun whale hunting again? We did have three brief sightings of a whale and a school of seals, but what I really wanted to see was the solitary tusk of a narwhal.

We sailed up into Isfjorden and into Billeforden, at the head of which lay the second Russian mining settlement, Pyramiden. The miners lived in functional yellow barrack blocks and went uphill to enter the coalmine. On the opposite shore there was a massive glacier. When the sun came out the green and blue ice sparkled. The ship turned and headed for Barentsberg where a crowd awaited the first big ship to arrive since the thaw, both climatic and political. It was July, 1993. We waited while a delegation of local dignitaries bargained and agreed what we should be allowed to see. Nothing much had changed since my previous visit. The ready supply of coal enabled the hothouses at the 'farm' to flourish and battery chicks, cows and piglets to thrive in dimly lit concrete sheds. A new 'hotel' had been built in 1988, which included a shop, post office and a bar where a friendly barmaid presided. It was evident that the hotel was seldom used and they were happy to serve any customers. An outdoor market, the Barentsberg Bazaar, had been hastily set up above the quayside, which sold badges, dolls, samovars, fur hats and travel books in Russian. It would have been churlish not to give these friendly people a few dollars for their limited stock. I was glad that every group we landed there bought something, even Barentsberg vouchers!

There was a very strange man in his thirties, who, after a couple of days, everybody tended to avoid sitting next to at meals. Not because he smelled but because he had a fixed belief that the world was going to end at the same time as the second coming and we should all be aware that the end was near. He began by saying: 'The angel of the Lord spoke to me at 3.16 am last Sunday advising that the second coming of Christ will be during the twenty-first hour of Saturday, 7 February, 2004. Notices to this effect were posted Luther-style on the doors of six places of local Christian worship and sent to the local and National Press. No answer has been the stern reply from any quarter. Next month's celebration of the Nativity will thus be the penultimate one. Rejoice and spread the news (to those you wholly trust).'

He had the courage of his convictions, gave up his job in the government office, sold his possessions and was travelling the globe spreading the news. The day came and went but the world was not ready for it. 'Mankind must now wait until Easter, 2010.' He ended a postcard with 'Good news! I have received heavenly answers to my prayers about the fulfilment of my precognitive dreams. Pass it on. Crispin.'

As we left Spitzbergen and were steaming slowly along through a field of pack ice a polar bear stood on a tiny piece of ice 10 miles from the shore. Later that afternoon a polar bear was seen on the starboard bow at least 20 miles from land, swimming strongly. On one occasion, after sighting eight bears, we entered a bank of fog. The ship pushed her way through a field of pack ice and slowed down to about one knot. It was a remarkable sight. We were surrounded, except at the stern, by hundreds of seals lying on every bit of broken ice. They did not move until the ship nudged past them. None of the experienced crew had ever seen anything like it. It was probably also the reason why we saw so many bears.

A visit to Franz Josef Land often needed the help of an icebreaker. It was a great relief to see the powerful searchlights of the atomic-powered *Tamyr* and tuck in behind her. We anchored off Cape Flora on Nortbruk Island, teeming with birds whose droppings have made it a fertile bed for Arctic flowers and moss. Only one wall of the hut built by Leigh Smith in the winter of 1881 remains. There are just a few metal hoops, all that remain from the barrels of salt, spices and curry. One wall has fallen into the sea and a few pieces of clothing remain. The skeleton of Jackson's 1895 hut and four octagonal store huts can be seen and bits of stove and pottery remain, but the timber was removed by Baldwin in 1904 and Sedov in 1913.

The Russians failed to provide us with two promised unemployed KGB men whose task it was to protect the party from polar bears. In despair we settled for a cook and a pianist who liked hunting.

On nearby Bell Island there was a hut created in 1881 on a low bank of shingle which had never been lived in. There were no birds to be seen, only a noisy colony of walrus. A party of Austrian scientists went too close and had to be rescued when their Zodiac (boat) was punctured by a walrus tusk.

Further east, above latitude 80.30, on Hooker Island there is a deserted Russian settlement built in 1913. Each wooden house has a small pier at the end of which there still is a privy. A shed on the water's edge contained two ancient tracked vehicles encrusted with snow and icicles. The tracks must have been just under a metre wide. Other huts contained batteries, trousers, books, barrels of lime and cement. There are a number of piles of stones, indicating graves, and a black cross made out of a propeller, probably an attempted winter landing on the ice.

Just offshore was Rubini Rock, a gigantic reddish volcanic rock rising sheer out of the water. The ever-friendly Russian helicopter pilots decided to lift the passengers to the top. There were no seat belts, no seats, just loose tubular kitchen chairs and no lifejackets.

The passengers walked around, opening windows to take pictures of polar bears. Having deposited a load on top of the rock the helicopter flew away. There was no radio communication; there was only one aircraft; there was no cold-weather survival gear or rations in case the aircraft broke down and we were cut off. The only way off the Rubini Rock was by helicopter or parachute.

The only person who fully appreciated our possible predicament if we were to have a breakdown was Commander Angus Erskine, RN. He successfully hid his concern from the passengers. Not far away, on Hooker Island, a strange rock lies on the seashore. It is about 2 metres in diameter and perfectly round. Dr David Taylor, who was with me, consulted a vulcanologist and a friend at the Institute for Polar Research in Bremerhaven. It was too big to be a volcanic bomb, unlikely to be a meteorite, because it would be unlikely to survive impact, he told me. It might be a concretion, which is formed chemically from iron carbonate radiating outwards from a nucleus. Or it might be an exfoliated rock produced by alternate cycles of heating and cooling, or glacial erratics, where the shape is produced by grinding and rolling. Whatever it was, the learned gentlemen had an open mind and the weathering effect is sometimes called *wollsack* in German. The mystery remains; the rock is still there, but only a Russian helicopter crew can find it again.

Right in the centre of the archipelago, tucked away from unwanted visitors, is Hayes Island. The settlement is built on the rim of a meteorite crater and is known as a weather station; however, the forest of radio masts round the crater indicates that there is also a communications purpose. About thirty people live there in wooden houses. They had not been paid for many months and were offering fossils and rocks, indeed anything they could spare, for dollars. There was one hut which called itself a nightclub, guarded by a hairy Siberian hound. A red-haired lady holding a rubber stamp and red inkpad barred our way until she could frank an envelope. She did not know when the post would leave, maybe in three months' time. In the valley there was a wrecked transport plane. The top 3 inches of the permafrost had given way and the aircraft was stuck in a sea of mud and ice. It was many months before the passengers had been able to leave the island in an icebreaker. It was with some relief that we rejoined the icebreaker and allowed the Russian sailors to wash the mud off our boots. The Captain of the icebreaker, Sergei Paschov, was determined that the British should take some close-up pictures of polar bears. He waited until all were back on the liner MV *Alla Tarasova* and then, having spotted a bear and her two cubs, used the icebreaker like a sheepdog to edge the bears towards the battery of cameras waiting on the bows of the *Alla Tarasova*. They crossed, leaving a distinctive trail of footprints in the snow-covered ice floe. Looking at my companions, I was relieved to see that a large lady, who had insisted on wearing a yellow floral pair of shorts when we went ashore on Spitzbergen, had taken my advice and put on trousers and two pairs of gloves. I had to explain to her that nobody was going to be impressed, let alone seduced, by her bare feet and purple toenails. She was foolish to risk certain frostbite.

Two years later, on a subsequent journey to Franz Josef Land, I asked whether we could visit Kheysa Island (Hayes) and was told that there was nothing there to see. Standing on a bridge, a quick glance at the chart showed a red dot where I remembered that the settlement had been located. The Iron Curtain had fallen again. Captain Anatoly Cherepanov made up for any disappointment by circling two whales which were sending spouts of water high into the air. They were accompanied by a very active group of seals. Everyone came on deck to wave goodbye to the icebreaker *Tamyr*, a stirring sight as the atomic-powered vessel overtook us at speed with an impressive bow wave which splashed over five walrus lying on a slab of ice. They have magnificent tusks which are used to pull themselves out of the water and for scratching the seabed for their favourite food, crustaceans. When the fighting for mates is over they lie on the ice farting and burping like the smoking room in an imaginary gentlemen's club after a heavy lunch. I treasure an Inuit-carved walrus tusk among a collection of green soapstone and crude bone carvings. They all have gentle curves and smooth surfaces and they can be passed round a dark shelter and felt by every pair of hands.

Among the handful of English speakers there was a Russian stewardess called Olga. She could understand what I said but had difficulty in plucking up courage to start a conversation if there was anyone else within earshot. She was a handsome lady with twinkling eyes, aged about thirty-five. When we visited Hooker Island she came ashore in one of the boats with members of the crew. She was wearing a long balldress. While we all wore gumboots and parka jackets, she wore a bright red pair of dancing shoes and a red plastic flower in her hair. Olga certainly had style.

A few days later I was checking through a mass of colour slides for a lecture to ensure none were upside down. She came into my cabin with her arms full of clean towels, no longer dressed as Calamity Jane of the early Western films. She stood silently watching, now and again saying 'good' and 'wonderful' or just 'ah so'. Then she said, 'You know I vos fighting in Afghanistan, two years.'

'No, I had no idea, Olga. What on earth were you doing?' I asked, then ventured to suggest, 'Were you an army nurse?'

Her reply was scathing. 'How can you imagine such a thing? I vos an Army Engineer, you know; roads, bridges, dugouts, minefields, bombs.' She paused to draw breath. 'EXPLOSIONS'. She sat down on my bed, clearly exhausted at the mere reminder of her time in Afghanistan.

'Then why do you want to do a job like this?' I asked.

'Oh, because it can be so much more exciting,' she whispered, dumping the towels on the floor and closing the door with her foot.

AFTERTHOUGHTS

Sadly, there were no more Olgas to give my travels a touch of the unexpected. It was always the people I met who made each journey worthwhile. I soon discovered that in every community there was a man in a humble position of authority who carried great respons-ibilities and the need to make bold decisions, at least in the eyes of his village. It might be the village constable or the local fisherman who was expected to be the first to take his dog sledge to test the thickness of the freshly frozen ice. The villagers all relied on his judgement.

Sometimes they might call for help from the best hunter when their flocks of sheep were being ravaged by a rogue wolf or pack of wild dogs. It might be a frontier guard who has to decide whether to allow a smuggler whom he knows pass and then risk the sack, or to arrest him and fear for the safety of his family. He often has lonely decisions to take, which to him and the community he serves appear momentous, but to an outsider who does not know the implications seem to be quite straightforward.

I have faint memories of other adventures, for instance going to a theatre in Macao, China, to see a cultural dance. My wife, Valerie, was the only woman among a sea of Chinese males, all wearing dirty mackintoshes. The star of the show was a young lady from East Germany called 'Kiki Railroad', who did a striptease dance on a red motorbike inside a glass water tank to much clapping and excited chatter.

In North Cyprus at Kantara Castle in the Kyrenia Mountains I was showing a busload of tourists round when a gentleman had a heart attack. There was not a telephone or house in sight. Not wish-ing to alarm the passengers, the tour manager, Fiona Guertz, and I put him on the back seat between us and said that he was not feeling well. I told the driver of the ancient bus to get us off the mountain fast. He got the message. At every hairpin bend the body, for he was by now dead, slid off the bench. I jammed his legs behind the struts of the seat in front. Then we thought, what if *rigor mortis* sets in before we get to a village? To cut a long story short, we had to drive round Famagusta trying to get someone to take the body off us!

Other memorable journeys include Brazil with its purpose-built capital city, Brasilia. All government offices were protected by a moat and all buildings stood on concrete pillars to protect them from hostile crowds. No wonder people preferred to live in Rio and enjoy its fabulous beaches.

In Kyoto, Japan, in the spring when the blossom was out, I was directed to where I could spend a penny and tucked myself away in the corner of a long building. I was horrified to be joined by four giggling ladies who came and stood on either side of me. There was a forced landing in Cameroon, a close call with a hippo at Juja, a farm in Kenya, butterflies in Brunei, the gold museum in Bogota, Indian embroidery in Guatemala and albatross and tiny penguins in New Zealand. It has all been wonderful and unforgettable. Travel breaks down barriers. I am sure if Daffodil had lived she would still be running ahead of me.

INDEX

195

de Verraillon, Admiral, 20
Denmark, 135, 139
Devon Island, 61
Doftana, 14, 21, 30, 31–2, 38, 44
Dollfus, Austrian Chancellor, 39
Douala, 127
Drepung Monastery, 113
Dreyfus, Collette, 94, 121
Dreyfus, Philippe Daniel, 79, 94
Dubai, 148
Dupont, Fifi, 43

Egede, Hans, 135
Egypt, 41
Eira, 184
Eisenhower, General, 147
Ekaterinburg, 16
Ekholm, Dr Nils, 163
El Dorado, 116
Elias, Gwyn, 43
Elizabeta, 16
Ellesmere Island, 61
Ellsworth, Lincoln, 167
Emperor Franz Joseph, 16
Empress of Canada, 173, 174, 176, 177
Enescu, George, 28
Erik the Red, 135
Erskine, Commander Angus, 161, 162, 169, 189
Erzurum, 126
Ethiopia, 41
Ettienne, Erich, 181
European Economic Community, 45
Exmouth, 31

Falklands War, 160, 179
Famagusta, 194
Fenton, Second Mate, 185
Ferdinand of Bulgaria, 15
First World War, 16, 39, 70, 80, 127, 173, 184
Foch, Marshal, 27
Focsani, 21
Forbidden City, 152

Fort Churchill, 60, 63
Fragrant Hill Hotel, 148, 149
Fram, 185
Franz Josef Land, 165, 185, 188, 190
French Foreign Legion, 41, 79
Frey Bridge, 89
Friendship Bridge, 103

Galatz, 14, 15
Gale, General Sir Richard, 126–7
Gallipoli, 173
Gardner, F.G., 166
Garter Parade, 127
Georgia, 27
German Democratic Republic (DDR), 85, 89
Ghika, Chouche, 44
Ghika, Tante Ephrosine, 18, 44
Ghika, Matila, 15, 20
Ghika, Radu, 43
Ghika, Sanda, 43
Gifhorn, 59
Giraud, Madame, 72
Giurgiu, 5, 8
Glen, Sir Alexander, 178–9
Godfrey, Lieutenant Colonel, 179
Golescu, General, 7
Gossley, Sir Savile, 185
Gothab, 136
Govorov, Senior Captain, 53–4, 56, 57
Govorov, Trudi, 53, 56, 58
Grand Duchess Olga, 16
Grand Duke Nicholas, 8–9
Gravesande, Laurens Storm van, 116
Great Wall of China, 151
Green Fjord, 171
Green Peace, 139
Green Shrimp discotheque, 119
Greenland, 133, 135, 139, 142
Grigorcea, Nicu, 43
Grigoresu, Paf, 43
Grivitza, 9
Guatemala, 194
Guertz, Fiona, 193
Guichard, Monsieur, 98